TRINITY BAPTIST CHURCH
501 NORTHSIDE DR.
CARROLLTON, GA 30117

Doc

By
Howard W. Roberts

McClain Printing Company
Parsons, West Virginia

1987

International Standard Book Number 0-9617971-0-X
Library of Congress Catalog Card Number 86-90702
Printed in the United States of America
Copyright © 1987 by Howard W. Roberts
Temple Hills, Maryland
All Rights Reserved

TABLE OF CONTENTS

Chapter	Page
Acknowledgements	V
Introduction	VII
1. Land of the Long Hunters	1
2. My Mother Was Away From Home When I Was Born	8
3. I Went Four Years to the Eighth Grade	22
4. We Didn't Show In That Ring	34
5. I've Had a Lot of Fun	46
6. I've Loved Every Minute of It	77
7. I'd Hate to Be the Richest Man in the Graveyard	134
8. A Lot Of 'Em Get Pulled Too Green	150
9. Each One Gets a Little Better	159
Bibliography	166

ACKNOWLEDGEMENTS

I am deeply indebted to many people for their assistance in the research and writing of this book. I am grateful to the Monticello Banking Company and especially to Charles Cowan for being interested in having this book written and for providing the financial resources that made it possible. My deepest gratitude is expressed to Mack and Alma Roberts who opened their lives to me so that I might learn about them and share their lives in print.

I greatly appreciate my family who were understanding of the time I had to be away from home researching this book and the time at home when I was away from them writing and rewriting. I am deeply indebted to Peggy Roberts and Sandra Gardner who proofread my manuscript and made helpful suggestions.

Written

I express my appreciation to the following people who shared with me written accounts of events and memories they recalled of encounters both personally and professionally with Dr. Mack Roberts. My thanks to Hattie Hurt, Edna Brooking DeLoach, Minnie Cross, Glenna Mae Catron, J. Estill Alexander, W. R. Denney, Corbin and Eva Lee Frost, Wilburn Jones, Ruby Jo Frost Denney, Betty W. Tuttle, Raymond Duncan, Brenda Orr, Neva Piercy, Lewis Kelley, Elba Matthews Wilhite, Lee and Barnett Abbott, Betty B. Wright, Amanda Roberts Dick, Ann Roberts Looney, Helen Roberts Dees, Marilyn Roberts Drake, Kathryn Ramsey, JoAnne Crain, Carolyn Needham, Nellie Coffee Adams, Delmar and Oakley Dalton, Joyce Logan, Gary Nell Hinton, Betty Roberts Ball, Doris Ingram Greene, Obie and Bulah Corder, Katie Lou Rector,

Ethel Hurt Sharpe, Marie Stearns, Netty Ann Bell, and Dale Logan.

Interviews

Many people assisted by talking with me personally and permitting me to interview them. Their sharing gave depth of content and breadth of comprehension about the life of Mack Roberts. I am grateful to Rick, Marilyn, and Mack Drake, Lonzo Bertram, Gifford Walters, Aleta Roberts, JoAnn Anderson, Mack Perkins, Lisle Roberts, Georgia Roberts, Mildred Tuttle, John Simmons, Ann Roberts Looney, Helen Roberts Dees, Tara, Mark, and Aimee Looney, Glenn Denny, Issac Hucaby, William Childers, Howard and Mildred Foister, JoAnne Crain, Lula Alred, Mr. and Mrs. Shelby Keeton, Lexie Williams, Mayo and Shirley Phipps, Lee Lacy and Maime Porter, Marie Blevins, Milton and Doris Roberts.

INTRODUCTION

Doctor Mack Roberts is a quiet, somewhat shy man of slight physical build. His thinning, dark hair is neither thinner nor lighter than it was forty years ago. About the only apparent sign of aging is the graying sideburns that jut out in front of his ear lobes. His movements and conversation are deliberate and unhurried. His interest and enjoyment of people is quickly evident through his dry humor and witty passing observations.

He has practiced medicine in Wayne County, Kentucky for more than fifty years. He is respected by people throughout the county and has contributed significantly to the quality of life there during the past half of a century. This book is his story, his life, his character, and tells how he has given of himself to the people of Wayne County.

Writing <u>Doc</u> has been a rich adventure for me because I have conversed with Doc, his family, his colleagues, his employees, and many of his patients. I have made house calls with him, and heard his side of telephone conversations with patients.

His life has touched eight decades in the twentieth century. He has seen and participated in phenomenal changes during his lifetime--from travel by horse and buggy to supersonic jets, from disease treatment by herbal home remedies to wonder drugs. He helped control smallpox and typhoid by visiting county schools and giving students vaccinations. He has participated in the eradication of polio with the use of Salk vaccine. He has seen the culture shift from rural to urban, but he has remained a country doctor who has cared for the health needs of people in both rural and city settings. He is the last doctor in Wayne County to make house calls, and in this regard, he may represent the end of an era.

Many names are used to refer to him in this book because to tell his story includes writing about his relationships with family, friends, and patients. He is Mack, Doctor Roberts, Doctor Mack, Doctor Mack Roberts, Doc Roberts, Doc, Daddy, Granddaddy, Poppie, and Uncle Mack. How people refer to him reveals insight into their relationship with him. For many people he serves a dual role. He is their physician and friend, he is their uncle and family doctor, or he is their doctor and business associate.

The testimony of Wayne Countians is that their quality of life has been enriched greatly because Doc has been on the job. This book is written with appreciation for Doctor Mack Roberts who was born, reared, educated, and practiced medicine in Wayne County, Kentucky.

Howard W. Roberts
Temple Hills, Maryland

LAND OF THE LONG HUNTERS

Nestled west of Appalachia, south of the Ohio Valley, east of the rolling prairies, and north of the Grand Ole Opry, is Wayne County, Kentucky. The plush meadows, surrounded by sparkling streams and rolling hills abundantly filled with wild game, created an inviting hunting ground for the Cherokee Indians. In 1770 when white hunters came to the territory, the Indians felt their land was being invaded. The long hunters, white men with long barreled rifles, were seldom conservative when they killed and used wild game. It was reported on one occasion by white men that their camp had been raided by Indians and 2,300 deerskins stolen.[1]

In 1774, when there was evidence of an Indian revolt, Daniel Boone and Michael Stoner were sent to the territory to warn settlers about the Indians. Boone and Stoner camped about five miles from Monticello.[2] Stoner liked the territory so well that he later returned and made his home there. A few years later, in May of 1779, the Virginia Assembly opened Kentucky to general settlement by survey, entry, and residence.

A road was marked and opened through the Cumberland Mountains known as the Wilderness Trail. With a travel route established, people began to move west into the county known as Kentucky, and in 1792 Kentucky was accepted as a separate state in the Union.

Settling Wayne County

By 1800 many Revolutionary Soldiers had settled in a section of the state that was named for the war hero Mad Anthony Wayne. Residents of the county have reflected a tranquil nature rather than the boisterous, stubborn attitude of the county's namesake. Wayne Countians have taken pride in their calm, easy going nature, have earned their livelihood from the land, and have felt a strong kinship with the earth.

In 1849 a large group of people migrated westward from Virginia into Kentucky. Whether they had heard of the gold rush and were on their way to get rich in California is unknown. However, it is known that several of the pioneers became ill and camped in Wayne County. When they recovered and were able to travel, some of them decided they had gone far enough, and Wayne County became home for them. Among those who decided to put down roots in Wayne County was Henry Roberts. Half a century later his great grandson, Mack Roberts, would be born in this county.

Henry Roberts fathered several children, among them Andrew Jackson Roberts. Andrew Jackson married Susan Clark, a relative of the explorer George Rogers Clark. This rustic and rugged couple lived in the eastern section of Wayne County in a brick house built by Samuel Ingram in 1837. The property where this house was located continues to be referred to as the old home place by the descendants of Andrew Jackson and Susan Roberts. Reference to Andrew Jackson by family members always includes his double name indicating the pride held by both him and them in his name.

Roberts Family History

Andrew Jackson Roberts was a farmer, a moonshiner, and a self taught blacksmith. He operated a still for many years, continuing the production during prohibition days. At one juncture when he thought the revenue officers were getting close on his trail and would destroy his still, he took a wagon, a team of oxen, and some of his sons with him. After dark they went over the mountain into McCreary County, loaded his still on the wagon and brought it to Oil Valley where he buried it under the chicken house. That made an excellent hiding place because the straw and shavings on the chicken house floor were moved aside when the hole was dug and then used to cover the fresh dirt after the still had been buried.

That was the end of Andrew Jackson's whiskey making but not the end of his whiskey drinking. He kept a bottle of moonshine in the stairwell at home, took at least one snort each morning, and gave samples to his grandchildren on many occasions.

During his early childhood, Mack Roberts lived with his family in his grandfather's house. He is one of the grandchildren who was given samples of Andrew Jackson's whiskey. "That was the worst tasting stuff I ever had," was Mack's assessment of the whiskey. "It burned all the way down. I don't see how anybody could stand to drink it." There were times, however, when Andrew Jackson mixed the whiskey with water, honey, and sugar. Mack said, "That was pretty good." Mack has never liked coffee and has drunk less than half of a cup in his whole life. He summarized this with the comment, "I've drunk more whiskey in my life than I have coffee," an unusual statement for a teetotaler.

Characteristic of the descendants of of the Roberts family has been to take politics seriously. Andrew Jackson's descendants have been staunch Republicans, and the commitment to the Republican Party can be traced to an event that happened to him during the Civil War. He was plowing corn when Rebel Soldiers came along. They roughed him up and stole his horse. Because the South and the Rebels were known to be strong supporters of the Democratic Party, Andrew Jackson, in protest to his treatment and having his horse stolen, changed political parties and most of his descendants down to the present are members of the Republican Party. However, Andrew Jackson's brothers remained members of the Democratic Party and so have many of their descendants.

In addition to farming, Andrew Jackson ran a blacksmith shop where he repaired buggies, buckboards, singletrees, horseshoes, and harnesses. A foreigner, meaning a stranger in the territory, Rhodes Rankin, was traveling in that part of the county and had a breakdown near the shop. He came to Andrew Jackson's blacksmith shop for assistance. While his buckboard was being repaired, another man present at the shop insulted Rhodes Rankin. Rankin responded by picking up a singletree and hitting his insulter over the head with it.

The previous night, May 13, 1874, a son, one of twelve children, had been born to Andrew Jackson and Susan Roberts, but a name had yet to be chosen. In those days it was the prerogative of the father to choose the name for his son. Andrew Jackson was so impressed with the rough and rugged manner of his foreign customer that he decided to name his son after him; therefore, Andrew Jackson's newest son was named Rhodes Rankin Roberts. Naturally, there are those who like to speculate that Rhodes' sometimes firey, stubborn disposition, and his unwillingness to take insults from anyone expressed kinship with the person for whom he was named. Susan Clark Roberts died in 1909, and it was not long before Andrew Jackson married Florence Phipps Dolen.

Verona (Rona) Clemmentine Vickery grew up in the Shearer Valley section of Wayne County. Before her marriage to Rhodes, Rona taught school at Burfield and boarded with Thursie and Celia Fairchild. Rona's father was Irvin Vickery. One of the favorite stories from his childhood was when he lay all day in the hot sun on top of the huge rock cliff at Flatt Springs on Beaver Creek and watched the Union Soldiers march down the road. The troops were being moved following the Battle of Mill Springs. Irvin felt trapped on the cliff, afraid if he moved the soldiers would see him, mistakenly assume him to be a spy, and shoot him.

On May 12, 1897, Rhodes Rankin Roberts and Verona Clemmentine Vickery were married and made their home on the third floor of the brick house with Rhodes' parents. They lived here for the first thirteen years of their marriage.

In 1901 oil was discovered on the B. E. Roberts land and on other nearby property. The B. E. Roberts' well, in its early days, produced 250 barrels per day. Because thousands of barrels of oil have been pumped from many productive wells through the years, this section of Wayne County has been known popularly as Oil Valley. Whether any official action was taken to give this name to the area is unknown, but for many years there was a post office with a sign that said Oil Valley Post Office. Apparently the cancellation of stamps with the Oil Valley postmark made the name official.

In 1910, Rhodes and his family moved further up the valley to the base of the mountain where he had bought land and an old log house from his brother, B. E. Roberts. B. E. retained the oil rights to the property. Rhodes and his family lived in the log house until 1915 when Rhodes had a new house built which cost $180, exluding the cost of the roof and chimney. In this house, Mack Roberts spent his middle childhood. On wintry mornings he would awaken with snow on his bed that had blown through the cracks, and in the spring his blankets would be covered with apple blossoms from the huge apple tree that stood in the yard. This house is still standing and is the home of Lisle and Ruth Roberts.

The quiet, unobtrusive Mack Roberts grew up in the peaceful setting of Oil Valley. He was guided by the loving care of rugged, pioneer spirited parents. Mack has cared for the medical needs of people throughout Wayne County and is referred to affectionately as "Doc."

Notes

[1]Augusta Phillips Johnson, <u>A Century of Wayne County Kentucky 1800-1900</u>. (Louisville: The Standard Printing Company, 1939), p. 4.
[2]Ibid.

Rona and Rhodes Roberts, Children and Grandchildren. Mack is in the center of the picture without a hat. The log house in the background is where the family lived from 1910 to 1915.

"MY MOTHER WAS AWAY FROM HOME
WHEN I WAS BORN"

With a twinkle in his eye and a chuckle in his voice, Doc likes to begin telling about his life by saying, "My mother was away from home when I was born." Although most people born today could make the same observation, that was not the norm in 1903. Obstetrics as a specialization in the practice of medicine is a recent development and having a hospital with a delivery room is even more recent for Wayne County. The hospital opened in December 1973. Only since then have many Wayne County mothers been away from home when their children were born.

The Birth of Roy Roberts

Rhodes and Rona Roberts' first son, Hobart, was born just ten months after their marriage and in less than two years Ottis, their second son was born. However, three years and five months passed before Roy's birth, their third of seven children.

In 1903 babies were born at home and neighbor women came to help with the birthing. Although Rona Roberts was pregnant and her due date was at hand, she traveled from Oil Valley to Cooper to see her father, Irvin Vickery, who was extremely ill. While she was visiting her parents, Rona's father died, and two days later, July 24, 1903 her son, Roy, was born.

During the first year of Roy's life a toll road was being built between Oil Valley and Monticello. The foreman on this construction project was an Irishman named McElroy. People in the

Roberts household began referring to the new infant as McElroy and then Mack Roy. Soon Roy was dropped and the youngster was called Mack. Because this was prior to the keeping of official records and the provision of birth certificates, which began in 1910, there was no problem changing an infant's name and the change did not cause any identity crisis for Roy, or Mack.

The length of time between the births of Ottis and Mack is significant for the emotional and psychological development of both. By the time Mack was born, Ottis was old enough to be playing independently as well as interacting comfortably with Hobart. This enabled Rona to spend more time with the new infant in the house and the time spent with Mack provided a psychological bonding between him and his mother that contributed significantly to him being a stable, well-adjusted, easy-going person. Mack was emotionally close to his mother and speaks with warm affection about her.

More than two and a half years passed after Mack's birth before Harry was born. This provided an adequate amount of time for Mack to become secure in the family before he had to make emotional room for a new brother and share the attention of his mother with another. Later this age difference created some natural competition between Mack and Harry in a variety of games and chores. One heated competitive event was getting dressed for school. If Mack won, then he had to fight Harry, because Harry couldn't stand to lose. One night Harry decided he was going to stay up so he could win. This strategy lasted about five minutes. Harry wanted badly to win, but his body wanted sleep worse. He finally took off his shoes, went to bed, and the next morning Mack won the dressing contest again.

Rona's Role

Rona was devoted to her family and seemed to work without ceasing. She lived an isolated life because of the requirements of being a farmer's wife and because of the distance the family lived from neighbors. During the spring and summer months she tended a large garden with the help of her children, raising many vegetables and fruits for spring and summer meals as well as canning them for the winter months.

Rona also raised turkeys and any money she made from selling turkeys was her spending money. The family raised chickens and any excess eggs were sold at the country store. The money was used to buy all the items the family needed from the store: sugar, coffee, and occasionally a few spices. All the other food items the family needed were produced on the farm. Corn and wheat were taken to the mill and an account was established. As the family needed corn meal and flour, they withdrew their corn and wheat as meal and flour.

An additional chore that Rona had was the daily job of preparing the noon meal for the farm work hands that Rhodes employed to help cultivate the land. Usually there were at least two seatings of eight men each for dinner. The number of work hands was reduced greatly during the winter months, especially after the tobacco had been stripped and taken to the market. Rona used the winter months to sew, make quilts, and knit socks.

During the early years of her marriage, Rona was the cook for the logging camp where Rhodes and several men were cutting timber. She would take her young children to the camp during the week, live in a shanty, and prepare the meals for the loggers. One day a logger came around the corner of the shanty and found Hobart, who was not yet two years old, face down in the water barrel. The logger pulled Hobart out of the water and revived him.

Rona was a soft-spoken, hard working woman who was sensitive to other people. Although Mack has easily identifiable characteristics of both of his parents, it is the consensus of those who knew both of his parents that Mack is more like his mother than his father.

Mack Perkins lived near the Rhodes Roberts family in the valley and often worked on the farm for Rhodes. He ate many work day meals at the Roberts house, and his mother, Dine Perkins, often worked for Rona, helping with cooking, canning, and laundry. Here is his description of Rona Roberts:

> She was a concerned woman, concerned about her home and her business. There never was a finer person ever lived than Mrs. Rona Roberts. She gave us food. We was awful poor. Didn't have no daddy. We lived off what people gave us. Rona was a gentle, kind, patient person. I have often used her as an illustration in my Sunday school class of what a Christian is to be.

Discipline

Rona often told her children that she and Rhodes disciplined them because they loved them. She would point out that parents who did not really care about their children were the ones who permitted their children to do as they pleased. Rona Roberts listened to her children's needs and concerns, and she was one to whom her children took their problems. Rona was a jolly woman who joked and teased with her family. She sang a lot and enjoyed humming and whistling when she worked, but her whistling days ended when she got false teeth. She was convinced her mother was happy about that because Rona's mother had never thought it was proper for a woman to whistle.

People were known to say to Rona, "You have six boys, and only one girl. I'll bet you spoil that girl." Rona would bristle a bit and reply, "I don't think any more of my girl than I do my boys!" Rona never left any doubt that she meant what she said.

Those of us living at the end of the twentieth century would assess life at the beginning of the century to be difficult and filled with hardships. That might have been Rona Roberts' assessment of life as well; however, she maintained a pleasant outlook and accepted her daily responsibilities with joy and thanksgiving, often communicating her happiness by whistling and singing as she worked.

The Authority Figure

Rhodes Roberts was an extremely hard worker and taught his sons the value of work. He was observant of life and learned the rock formations, the trees, shrubs, and wildlife as an ecologist learns them today. He was especially skilled at finding jobs for every member of the family and for assigning jobs to individuals that fit their ages and abilities. As each child got older he was given additional and more difficult assignments, but never to the point that he became overly frustrated or discouraged because of the task. During the school years when the boys would return to the fields during school breaks,

Rhodes would involve them in a full day of work gradually, beginning with a couple of hours the first day and increasing the number of hours of work each day until they were once again working a full day like everyone else.

All the boys worked on the farm plowing the land, planting crops, thrashing wheat, cutting corn, putting barley and wheat in sheaths, and putting loose hay in the barn. This was before the days of haybailers, but progress came to the Roberts farm when Rhodes bought a fork for the barn loft. This fork fit on a track and could be lowered to the wagon where the hay was and lift a huge amount of hay into the loft. Those working in the loft would push the hay fork along the track to the place where they wanted the hay dropped. Then they would release the fork, and using pitch forks, would spread and stack the hay.

Rhodes worked for a living and expected everybody to work a full day. The work day on the Roberts farm was from sunrise to sundown, and the pay was seventy-five cents per day. Once Mack Perkins was ten minutes late getting to work and Rhodes sent him home saying, "When I pay a man for a day's work, I expect him to work all day. Go on back home. Come back tomorrow when you can work all day."

Rhodes enjoyed working and continued to work many years after others his age had retired. One day when Rhodes was in his middle seventies he was planting corn. A neighbor came by, stopped at the fence row and yelled across the field, "Rhodes, if I were as old as you, I'd do just what I wanted to do."

Rhodes responded "That's what I'm doing-- planting corn."

Rhodes Roberts had high ideals for himself and others. He expected people to live up to his ideals. One of his mottoes was "Each generation must keep up the good name." He was willing to tell people what he thought whether they wanted to know or not. Rhodes always enjoyed telling and hearing jokes, especially ones that would be considered a bit risque´. And he delighted in being able to embarrass people by teasing them in front of others.

He was the authority figure in the family and was fair-minded and even-handed in the decisions he made regarding family situations. He was a community minded person and was deeply devoted to his church in the valley.

Church Was Important

To understand the Roberts family requires an understanding of the Baptist denomination of which at least four generations of Roberts have been members. When Rhodes and Rona Roberts married and began their family in the valley there was no Baptist Church in that community. Rhodes was a member of the Big Springs Baptist Church which was in Burfield, about five miles over the mountain from where he lived. For several years Rhodes was the song leader for the worship services. He had a tuning fork and took it with him to set the pitch for the congregational singing. Lonzo Bertram, a young man in the church at that time, remembered Rhodes striking the tuning fork to the pulpit and holding it up in order for people to get the right pitch. Lonzo commented, "We didn´t have one of those things in our hollow."

Church services were held one weekend each month, but Sunday school met every Sunday. On the weekend each month when church services were held, a business meeting would be conducted on Saturday morning and then worship services would be held Saturday evening, Sunday morning, and Sunday evening.

Horseback was Rhodes´ method of transportation, and as late as 1956 he was seen riding his horse in Monticello. He rode horseback to church, and as the boys got old enough to go with him to church, Rhodes took them on his horse. Members of the Big Springs Baptist Church remember seeing Rhodes come over the mountain, out of the woods, riding his horse with one boy in front of him and one or two riding behind him.

When people in the community where the Roberts family lived began collecting money to build the Elk Spring Valley Baptist Church, Rhodes gave Trave Gibson $10 for the church, a generous donation in 1912. Eli Correll became the first pastor of the church, but Rhodes continued to ride over the mountain to Big Springs to attend church for a couple of years. Later he moved his membership to the Elk Spring Valley Baptist Church, and his brother, Rueben Roberts, served for a while as the pastor. Rueben lived at Oak Grove and rode horseback the twenty miles from Oak Grove to Elk Spring Valley to conduct services once each month. In those days it was considered a sin for the preacher to receive money for his work. However, Rueben did tell about being given fifty cents one year for his services.

Rhodes Roberts was the first Sunday school superintendent of the Elk Spring Valley Baptist Church and taught a Sunday school class as well. His class was known as the Card Class because each student was given a card with a picture on one side and a Bible verse on the other. The Card Class was for boys and girls between eight and twelve years old. One year when the church was looking for Sunday school teachers, Rhodes commented, "Well, I don´t know what the church is going to do about the other classes, but nobody is going to get my Card Class."

Apparently Rhodes was possessive of his positions because he was the only Sunday school superintendent the Elk Spring Valley Church had had at the time of his death in 1956. By then the congregation had built a new building but had not had a service in it, and Rhodes' funeral was the first service held in their new building.

Rona Roberts also was devout in her religious faith and maintained her membership in the Christian church throughout her life. On many occasions Rona attended the Elk Spring Valley Baptist Church and the Elk Spring Valley Church of Christ. She did not go to church as regularly as Rhodes because for many years there was at least one small child to be cared for at home. It was neither wise nor convenient to ride horseback with an infant four or five miles to church. She also considered it her responsibility to have a multi-course, hot Sunday dinner prepared and ready for her family when they returned from church. She would have Lisle stand at the top of the hill and look for his father and brothers coming from church. When he saw them coming out of the woods, he would run to the house and tell Rona. She would put the homemade bread in the oven so that it would be baked and ready to serve warm by the time Rhodes and the older boys got to the house and sat down to dinner.

Operating the Farm

The family owned between thirty and forty cattle and about one hundred hogs. The hogs were raised on the mast, which meant they lived in the woods and ate acorns for their main food supply. It was necessary for someone to go into the woods periodically, call the hogs, and feed them some corn; otherwise, the hogs would become wild. The family butchered eight or ten hogs each year, cured the hams and bacon, made sausage, and rendered four or five stands of lard that provided the grease needed for cooking. "That was good for our cholesterol level," Mack observed. The family also made their own soap.

Breakfast at the Roberts household was a warm, enjoyable time. It followed the morning chores of checking the livestock, milking the cows, and opening the chicken house. Someone had to take the milk to the spring to refrigerate it. While Rhodes and the boys were taking care of these jobs, Rona and Joyce, the only daughter and the youngest of the seven children, were preparing a hot breakfast usually consisting of bacon or sausage and eggs or fried chicken, gravy, and always plenty of hot homemade biscuits. While breakfast was being eaten, the family related warmly to each other and shared in decision making regarding family matters. Breakfast was also the time when work plans and job assignments were made for the day.

The Trio

Mack and Ottis seemed especially close as young boys and teenagers. Rona said that Mack was dependable. If she asked him to do something it was not necessary to prod him. (The same could not be said of all the children.) Rona often remarked that Mack was especially good to look after the younger children when they were little.

Hobart, Ottis, and Mack were an energetic trio who played, worked, and hunted together as children. Their play time usually found them competing in marbles, checkers, or dominoes, making cob horses, riding stick horses, battling each other in a cob fight out at the barn, or making bows and arrows. Sprouts from sourwood trees made good arrows. They also had great fun with a gum sling. However, if any of them knocked down a goose with a sling, he was in trouble and the sling would be confiscated for a few days.

These three boys were skilled hunters and enjoyed searching for animals for food and fur. They were going to the woods together to hunt before they were teenagers, and there were no serious injuries or accidents. Apparently they observed excellent safety rules, were lucky, or perhaps a little of both. They kept traps set and checked them every day. They were permitted to hunt every day except Sunday. Because Sunday was to be a day of rest, they were to rest from hunting and give the animals a day of rest too.

This hunting trio was especially interested in fur bearing animals, including raccoons, rabbits, foxes, polecats, and ermine. An ermine is a weasel whose coat turns white during the winter. They often sold the pelts they collected to a company in Cincinnati, Ohio. The money they received from their hunting expeditions was theirs to use as they wished. This was about the only way they had of obtaining any spending money.

These three young trappers came up with an idea of how to catch more animals when they were hunting, especially those that would run into their holes for protection from the trigger trio. They bought a smoke gun and used it to smoke out the animals that tried to hide in their burrows and holes. The smoke gun worked well, but the plan didn´t because the animals preferred to suffocate instead of coming out to be caught by these three.

The daily responsibility of Hobart, Ottis, and Mack was to provide the firewood for the day. This was a much easier job in the summer than in the winter. The only wood needed during the late spring and summer was to provide fuel for the wood cook stove where Rona prepared all the meals and canned fruits, jellies, and vegetables. However, the winter need for wood required much more work. Wood was burned in the fireplaces, the only means for heating the house.

The boys cut small trees and used calves trained to yoke to haul or pull trees from the thickets to the wood yard. Then they used a cross cut saw to cut up the wood. As the younger brothers got old enough, they helped with this chore and often there was competition between two pairs of brothers to determine who could saw the most wood in the shortest amount of time. What was frustrating to these older three was for them to work several hours getting the wood ready, only to have everyone in the family burn it up that night. They had to start over the next morning. Those who did not cut the wood gave little thought about how much wood they were burning, but the three woodcutters were conservative when they put logs on the fire.

In addition to the outside chores, there also were responsibilities inside the house that each member of the family shared. Two of the jobs Mack most often did around the house were to dry the dishes and to cut up the chicken for frying.

Rona Roberts was a quiet woman who was interested in her children and their well being. She spent time with them after school assisting them with their homework and encouraging them to earn an education. She was an excellent letter writer, and when one of her children was away from home for an extended period of time she wrote that child every Sunday afternoon. Her kind, gentle nature conveyed her love and care for her children. She died on Valentine's Day in her seventy-fifth year.

Rhodes Roberts was a stalwart farmer and logger who was somewhat abrupt in communicating with others. He enjoyed riding his horse through the woods or anywhere else that he wanted to go. It was his method of transportation throughout his life. Just a few days before he died he took his horse out to the field and turned it out to pasture. It was as if he knew he would not ride again, and he didn't. He died in the Fall of 1956 at the age of eighty-four.

Rhodes and Rona Roberts created a happy, harmonious climate in which to nurture and nourish their family. They instilled in their children the importance of telling the truth, of treating everybody fairly and equally, of being kind to people, and of working for a living.

Naturally, Mack has characteristics of his parents. He has the humor, stubbornness, and optimism of his dad combined with the gentleness, quietness, and kindness of his mother. Mack evaluated his childhood family experiences with this assessment, "It was a pretty good living. We didn't have any luxuries but we got by."

Mack Roberts, age two, sitting in his wagon.

Left to right, Hobart, Joyce, Harry, Ottis, Mack, and Lisle Roberts.

"I WENT FOUR YEARS TO THE EIGHTH GRADE"

Both Rhodes and Rona Roberts supported their children in their pursuits of education. Their seven children attended the Oil Valley School, a three and a half mile walk from their house. The children made that walk every school day from the first of July until Christmas. The schoolhouse had one room, one teacher, and students were distributed from grades one through eight. As many as sixty-five students would begin the school year, but the attrition rate was high and in a normal year only twenty students would still be attending at the close of school in December. The school day began at 8:00 a.m. and ended at 4:00 p.m. with three recesses, half an hour in morning, an hour for lunch, and half an hour in the afternoon.

Rona instilled in her children the importance of getting an education. When Hobart, the oldest child, began high school at age eighteen, he brought books home to read for reports in English class. Beginning with these and continuing as her other children went to high school, Rona would read whatever books her children brought home from school for their homework. Because of Rona's interest in learning and there being no easily accessible libraries, she subscribed to several magazines and to <u>The Saint Louis Globe Democrat</u> or <u>The Kansas City Star</u>, which were weekly publications.

Having taught school before she married, Rona's interest in learning and her desire for children to learn carried over into her family life. She helped her children with their lessons and encouraged them to read. Much of her reading encouragement was conveyed through her own reading. Children learn what they live, and Rona's children learned from her that reading and learning were important.

Elementary School

Mack lacked twenty three days being six years old when he entered the first grade. Charles O. Ryan was the teacher at the Oil Valley School that year. During the day, Hobart went outside to the drinking fountain, a dipper in a bucket, to get a drink. Mack decided he needed a drink too. He jumped up and ran toward the door to follow his oldest brother. Mr. Ryan called to him, "Young man, come back here and walk out of the room." Mack did as he was told. That afternoon he walked home from school and did not walk back to school until the next year! The event was upsetting to Mack, and his parents decided that he was too young to walk seven miles each day to go to school.

Mack started to the first grade for the second time in 1910 just before his seventh birthday and continued through the eighth grade without missing a year. It was not unusual for children to go to school for two or three years and then drop out, often because the parents needed them to help with the farm responsibilities.

Amanda Lovelace was Mack's second first grade school teacher. Mack said of Miss Lovelace, "I believe I was one of her pets." One cold winter morning, she was having difficulty getting the fire in the stove to burn. Mack suggested that Miss Lovelace name the fire for her boyfriend and that would make it burn.

Mack's school teachers liked him, often telling his parents what a fine student he was.

He was not one to get into scrapes, to be a prankster, or cause much uproar. He was well balanced, ready to calm down other students if they seemed to be getting out of hand. Mack enjoyed going to school, and once received a barlow knife worth fifteen cents for having perfect attendance during that school year.

About the only thing that Mack didn't like about school was having to memorize poetry. Whenever there was a poem in the lesson, he knew they would have to memorize it. This was his complaint:

"The teachers then weren't very good. They didn't explain what the poems meant. They just made you memorize them."

This expectation to memorize caused him to dread going to school on the days that recitation would be required. The dread of recitation also inspired Mack to find ways to prevent him from attending school on those days. Although he was creative in his search for ways to miss school, none of them ever worked out well.

> One day on the way to school when I was going to have to recite a poem, I got a stomach cramp and went back home. Another time I tried to catch a fly to swallow because I had heard that if you swallowed a fly, it would make you sick. If I were sick, I wouldn't have to recite. But it didn't work. I never could catch a fly.

Mack enjoyed school so much that he went to the eighth grade four consecutive years. When he completed the eighth grade the first time and was ready for high school, Mack's dad would not permit him to go to high school because he needed him on the farm. Besides, by the time the boys were old enough for high school they were strong enough to put in a hard day of labor from sunrise to sunset. Another reason for delaying permission for the boys to go to high school was so the younger brothers could have some time to grow older and stronger and help do the work when an older brother went to high school. What Mack did was to continue going to school on days that he was not needed on the farm or on days when the weather prevented working in the fields. As a result he went to the eighth grade four years.

Mack's first trip beyond Wayne County occurred during his sixteenth year. Through his 4-H project of raising hogs, Mack won an all expense paid trip to the State Fair in Louisville. He rode with some of the 4-H sponsors to Burnside to catch the train. As they rounded the bend near the train station, Mack saw the train leaving. He was sad and disappointed because he thought they had missed the train. He had no idea there was more than one train each day that came through the station. His spirits were lifted when he learned they had not missed their train. This trip to Louisville was only the first of many travel adventures that Mack has embarked on throughout his life. Traveling became one of his great joys in life.

High School

Apparently, the eighth grade took to Mack as well as he took to it. His high school classmates commented about what an outstanding student Mack was. Andrew York said Mack was a whiz in math in high school and commented:

> I don't know if the teachers ever counseled with him and asked

his advice about the class, but if I had been the teacher, I sure would have. He knew his stuff.

Mack entered Monticello High School in 1921 because it was the closest high school to Oil Valley. He completed the diploma requirements in three and a half years and graduated with the class of 1924. Mack drove a little horse and buggy to town each day to attend high school and left it with his Uncle Woolford Vickery who lived on South Main Street. One day Uncle Woolford, a big man weighing more than 300 pounds, needed to go on an errand across Morris Hill. He decided to ride Mack's little black horse, but he was too much for the horse. The horse had a heart attack and died on the way over Morris Hill. When Mack returned from school he had only harness and a buggy to get him home. Mack was able to get another horse and continue his education.

Mack was older than most people in his graduating class of fourteen students because he spent four years in the eighth grade. In 1986, six of his high school classmates were still living, but he was the only man. He continues to ask Lula Alred, "When are we going to have that class reunion?"

Mack was the Business Manager of The Pilot, the high school annual, and his favorite expression, according to The Pilot, was, "Subscribe to the annual." The phrase that Mack's fellow high school classmates used to describe him was, "Carries the world on his shoulders." That may have been perceptive by his classmates because of the seriousness with which he approached his studies. The phrase may also have been an attempt to identify the sensitivity that Mack seemed to have toward other people and their circumstances in life.

Mack came to the city school from the county and graduated as valedictorian of his class. Lula Gamblin Alred enjoyed teasing him, claiming if he had not come to school, she would have gotten all the honors. During his high school years Mack was a member of the Athenian Literary Society and had roles in at least two plays. He became known as "Papee" because of his role in one play, and in <u>Borrowed</u> <u>Money</u> he played the part of Charles C. Vautrey, a home town success. Apparently he took the part to be type casting for his life. When a high school senior, Mack was asked what he wanted to be and he replied, "Great." He has become great in the genuine meaning of the word because the person who desires greatness must become the servant of others, and Mack Roberts has devoted his life to serving the medical needs of the people of Wayne County, Kentucky. His classmates anticipated that he would be great someday, but with a different definition of greatness, because it was their opinion that Mack was most likely to become a member of Congress.

His classmates also had some concerns about Mack such as, "We wonder why Mack Roberts never fell in love." There was at least one occasion when Mack got into trouble because the record shows that on January 19, 1924, Mack Roberts was asked to throw out his chewing gum. And only in high school did Mack finish second to anybody. He was voted second to Ed Dodson as the most brilliant, and second to Virginia Baker as the most likable student. Mack began grade school for keeps in 1910 and graduated from Monticello High School in 1924.

College

Mack was influenced to go to college after attending a career day presentation at Monticello High School. There were people representing several colleges at that program. He heard Dr. Wright, a Cumberland College representative, say, "Life might have more abundance. It can be sweeter than honey and the drippings of honeycomb." Those words stuck in Mack's ears and caused him to give serious consideration to going to college. There was no precedent in his family for college, but he became the first member of his family to attend college. Several years later after he had finished college and paid off some of his debts, he loaned money to his younger brothers and sister so they also could go to college.

Because of the comments of Dr. Wright, Mack was influenced to go to Williamsburg, Kentucky, to enroll in Cumberland College. Mack had no money to go to college. He and his brother, Ottis, owned a mule in partnership, and Ottis paid Mack three or four times what his half of the mule was worth to provide him with some money. Mack also had driven mules hauling logs making $7.50 per week. The night before he left for college his dad asked him how much money he had.

Mack responded, "Forty dollars." Rhodes said, "I have a two dollar bill in my pants pocket. If you'll give me a one, I'll give you the two dollar bill."

Mack made the trade and left the next day for college with forty-one dollars in his pocket.

Getting to Williamsburg was no simple matter. First Mack got a ride to Monticello where he caught the stagecoach, which he rode twenty miles to Burnside. In Burnside he boarded the train and road it to Liberty. There he got a ride with someone to Williamsburg.

After he arrived in Williamsburg, his forty-one dollars did not last long. He expressed his concern to some of the administrative officials at the college, and was told to see a man about a loan, and was given instructions to his house, and he went there.

> I had never seen such a huge house in all my life. I must have walked past it five or six times before I ever got up the nerve to go to the door and knock. Finally, I did get up my courage and knocked. I was greeted warmly and after we had talked awhile I learned that the man's wife was from Monticello. That helped!

Mack did receive a loan which greatly assisted him financially. He paid back the loan after he completed his college education.

In 1985 Mack gave $10,000 to Cumberland College to set up a loan like the one he received when he entered college. Students who receive the loan are to repay the money after they complete college. This system provides a perpetual loan available to students who enter college with financial needs like Mack had in 1924.

When Mack enrolled in college, Cumberland was a junior college. Gifford Walters, a classmate of Mack at Cumberland, said:

> Mack was a serious student, much more serious than I. I was there to play basketball, but Mack Roberts was there to get an education and he did. He also knew how

to take care of himself and his things. He put his trousers between the mattress and box springs to press them and to keep them from wrinkling.

Upon completing Cumberland College, Mack entered the University of Louisville and spent two uneventful years there earning his bachelor's degree. The main event which occurred during these two years was the indebtedness Mack incurred to pay for his education. Following his graduation from the University of Louisville, Mack taught school for a year at Griffin in Wayne County. His reason for teaching was to earn money to repay the money he had borrowed. On another occasion he taught school from July until September when the fall semester began at medical school.

Medical School

The way Mack got into medicine is at least a two part story. His family's doctor was Dr. O. M. Carter. Near the time of high school graduation Dr. Carter invited Mack to come by his office. He gave Mack a fountain pen as a graduation gift, and while Mack was in his office Dr. Carter asked,

"Have you ever thought about going into medicine?" Mack admitted to him that he had not really thought about that. Dr. Carter encouraged him to consider it for two reasons.

"First, you will be able to live a little better than the average person. Second, and more importantly, you will be able to bring sunshine where the cloud of despair has hovered over a family."

This encouragement by his own physician had an effect on Mack and caused him at least to think about becoming a doctor. However, Mack was a good student in mathematics and considered entering the engineering field. His desire to become an engineer lasted until he got into analytical geometry at Cumberland. Text books were unavailable during the first two weeks of the course. By the time the books had arrived, Mack was sunk. This experience, along with the encouragement he had received from Dr. O. M. Carter, caused Mack to decide to study medicine.

While Mack was in medical school Rona washed and ironed his shirts. Then she packed them neatly in a black valise, fastened the outside straps and mailed them to him in Louisville. Certainly this act of love exemplifies the warm support that Mack received from his mother for the grand effort he was giving to obtain an education. This expression of support helped Mack survive the stress and strain of medical school.

During his junior and senior years in medical school, Mack worked as an on call physician in the emergency room of Louisville City Hospital. His junior year he received room, board, laundry and thirty dollars per month as payment. His senior year he received room, board, and laundry, but no thirty dollars. The reason for the difference was that the junior student had to go on ambulance calls, but the senior student did not. The work schedule involved being on call twenty-four hours and off twenty-four hours. He was permitted to sleep between calls. It was during this experience that Mack developed the life long ability he has maintained to be able to fall asleep anywhere at anytime he needs to rest. One of his favorite sleeping spots for these forty winks is in the middle of the floor.

By the time Mack completed medical school he had incurred a debt of $5,000, which at that time would have been enough money to buy any two farms in Wayne County. Mack's indebtedness at the end of medical school was equivalent to a $300,000 debt in 1986.

After completing medical school in 1932, Mack served as Wayne County Health Officer until the summer of 1938. In July of 1938 he began a year of internship at St. Joseph's hospital in Lexington. Internships are not required for people to be qualified as doctors, but it is common practice for doctors to do them.

In the latter half of 1939, Dr. Roberts began his private medical practice in Monticello, This by no means suggests that he ended his education in 1939. He has continued to learn the art of practicing medicine and has done a remarkable job of keeping abreast of his profession by reading medical journals and attending regional, state, and national medical meetings. Humility, which means to be teachable, is one of Dr. Roberts' outstanding qualities. Therefore, the education of Mack Roberts will continue throughout his life because he is an observer of life and constantly open to learning.

Mack Roberts' graduation picture from Cumberland College, 1926.

Dr. Mack Roberts upon graduation from the University of Louisville Medical School, 1932.

4
"WE DIDN'T SHOW IN THAT RING"

On a bright sunshiny day during the fourteenth year of Mack's life as he was walking home from school, he met Mr. and Mrs. Joe Dolen riding in their buggy. Mrs. Dolen was carrying their newest baby in her lap. Mack took one look at the baby and said, "That's the girl I am going to marry." This romance really didn't happen quite like that, but this was the first time Mack saw Alma.

Matchmaking

Being a handsome, eligible bachelor doctor resulted in a variety of people wanting to try their hands at matchmaking for Mack. Mack took these efforts in stride, went about his medical work professionally, and brushed off the matchmaking efforts with a bit of humor.

A difficult situation did develop while Mack was serving his internship at St. Joseph's Hospital in Lexington. His brother, Kermit, developed blood poisoning as a result of an infected hair follicle. Because antibiotics had not been developed, the primary treatment was to bleed patients who suffered from blood poisoning and to cool them with cold towels and ice, hoping the body would outlast the infection. Kermit was taken to St. Joseph's Hospital, a hundred miles away, for this treatment, but it did not work for him. He died at the age of twenty-nine, leaving his wife Bessie and four daughters. Bessie was pregnant at the time, complications in her pregnancy developed, and she was hospitalized at St. Joseph's. Her baby was stillborn.

After Kermit died and Bessie lost her baby, several people tried to play matchmaker between Bessie and Mack. They concluded that Mack was the natural person to become the father of Kermit's children and husband of his widow. While Bessie was hospitalized a nun talked to her about what a good husband and father Mack would make. Then the nun talked to Mack about Bessie's need for a husband and his nieces' need for a father. She emphasized what a natural choice he was. But Mack was wise enough to know that a marriage is built on much more than duty and obligation. He never considered dating or marrying Bessie because no relationship of affection and commitment ever developed. This whole situation created tension between Mack and Bessie, but Mack resisted the pressure and made the right choice for the right reasons.

After Kermit's death Mack did accept responsibility as legal guardian for his nieces who were seven, five, three, and eighteen months old when their dad died. Mack provided for them emotionally and financially until each became an adult at age eighteen. As their guardian, Mack took Kermit's life insurance money and invested it in war bonds. This was all the money Betty, the oldest daughter, had to pay for college, and it paid for one year of business college. The amount invested was $500 and in twelve years it earned $160 interest.

Soon after Mack became the children's guardian, he bought them a pony named Bill and a buggy, but Bill died soon after he gave him to them. Mack had a pump installed in their well, and purchased a kerosene refrigerator for the house. Later, after he and Alma were married, he brought home groceries every Saturday night to take to Bessie and her children on Sunday afternoon.

In addition to serving as the guardian for Kermit and Bessie's children, Mack also was their physician. Gary Nell Hinton, one of the daughters, remembers, not so fondly, that Uncle Mack gave them their vaccinations. She recalled hiding from him on Sundays because that was when he would go to see his parents, check his mother's blood pressure, and give his nieces, who lived nearby, any vaccinations they needed.

Another health care need was when Betty mashed her finger cracking hickory nuts and then the cat scratched it. It became infected and Mack had to lance it. The pressure was so great that when Uncle Mack lanced it the pus hit the ceiling in his office. Betty was crying terribly and Mack threatened to spank her because she was crying so much. She was always a little scared of him after that.

Uncle Mack seemed always to know when report card day was in the Wayne County school system. He would be waiting at the corner in front of Rankin's Drugstore when the bus from Wayne County High School stopped and his nieces would get off the bus. He would reward them with a dollar for each A.

In 1948, Bessie's home burned. Uncle Mack and Aunt Alma brought each of the four girls four dresses from the dress shop that Aunt Alma owned and operated. That was a big help to them because school was to begin soon. Uncle Mack remained faithful in his guardian responsibilities until all four girls were grown.

Alma's Childhood

The infant that Mack saw during his fourteenth year grew up to be a beautiful woman. Alma Dolen was the sixth of seven children born to Joe and Estella Dolen. There were three boys and four girls. Alma was born at Griffin where her father owned a store, operated a farm, and worked as a driller in the oil fields with a productive lease. Alma's mother was the disciplinarian in their family, which meant she had the primary responsibility for rearing the children.

As a child Alma worked piecing quilts, catching geese, and helping pick them. From her earliest memory, Alma was an avid reader and even figured out a way to read while she churned butter. She attended the Oil Valley School through the eighth grade, and Harry Roberts was her last teacher there. Near the end of her eighth school year the handsomest man she had ever seen came into the school building to see Harry. She commented to her friend about how handsome that man was. The man was Mack Roberts, Harry's brother, who was a student in medical school at that time.

Courtship

The following year Alma attended high school in Monticello. During that year she and her sister, Shirley, Joyce Roberts, and Shirley Stearns rode to Monticello with Roy Orr. But by her sophomore year, Mack Roberts had completed medical school, and lived with his parents in Oil Valley. He was the Health Officer for Wayne County, had bought a car, and drove to his office in Monticello each day. It became convenient for Alma to ride to Monticello each day with the handsomest man she had ever seen, although few if any vibrations of affection were communicated then. They did not begin dating until several years later. There are those in Wayne County who remember them riding together and assume that their courtship began then.

Mack was the most eligible bachelor in the county, maybe the state, and the daily travel with Alma contributed to them getting to know each other. However, their dating did not begin until after Alma had attended Cumberland College for one year, and transferred to Western Kentucky State Teacher's College where she changed her major to Home Economics. Although Alma had enough credits for a college degree, she did not have enough of the requirements for a diploma. She became the teacher at the Jennings Hollow School near Windy, Kentucky, where she had twelve students in eight grades.

During the time Alma was the Jennings Hollow teacher she attended a teachers' conference in Somerset. To facilitate her traveling to Somerset she spent the nights with her sister and brother-in-law in Monticello. She was on her way to a movie when "Mack waylaid me. That's how we started dating." And as Alma enjoys adding, "It had taken Cupid a long time to do his work."

When Mack and Alma began dating he was living at the Cooper Hotel which later became known as the Sutton Hotel, located behind the Monticello Banking Company's main office next to where the Post Office is located today. Mack was the Wayne County Health Officer, but soon resigned to do a year of internship at St. Joseph's Hospital in Lexington, Kentucky. Then he returned to Monticello to begin his private medical practice and continue his courtship of Alma Dolen.

Mack was known to watch from his office for Alma to appear on the street in Monticello on Saturday, the day when everyone came to town. Then he would time a trip to the Post Office, located across the square from his office, so that he would happen to meet Alma and ask her if he could stop by to see her that evening at her home.

Most evenings when he visited Alma at home he would leave between eight thirty and nine o´clock, which was frustrating to Alma. She didn´t understand why he didn´t stay later, but he seemed especially sensitive that he not wear out his welcome with her parents.

Mack was then and is now extremely handsome to Alma. He was a bit shy and older. She liked older men and she considered the boys her own age to be frivolous. There was nothing silly about Mack. She liked his maturity. She knew his family and background, having gone to school to Harry and with Kermit, Lisle, and Joyce.

In Mack´s travels and the thousands of homes he has been in, the only place he has had any difficulty with a dog was at the Dolens when he dated Alma. Alma´s sister, Mamie, had a dog named Old Sport. Actually, she had three successive dogs with this same name. The first Old Sport never did like Mack, and he passed on his dislike to his successors. Each Old Sport always was after Mack´s heels, even after he and Alma married, and each dog continued to dislike Mack until its dying day. The fact that Mack growled at and pestered each dog probably contributed to the dislike displayed by Old Sport.

Any courtship reaches a critical point when the seriousness either increases or wanes. In Mack and Alma´s case the longer they dated the more serious their relationship became. For a long time Mack did not think the relationship would get beyond being good friends and dating occasionally because of their strong differences in politics, she a Democrat and he a Republican, and because of their strong religious differences. Alma was a faithful member of the Church of Christ and Mack was just as faithful to the Baptist Church. On one of their dates as they were discussing issues that come between couples, the subject of religion came up. Alma stated, "I would never let my church come between me and the man I love." Mack said of this, "At that moment, "I knew I was in business." The political and religious differences have remained throughout their marriage. They continue to attend separate churches regularly and to support both churches financially. They have had many discussions, debates, and arguments through the years over religious doctrine. Their three daughters remember many of those discussions.

The girls also remember going to church with each of their parents. Helen recalls that when she went to church with her mother she was given a penny to put in the offering, and when she went with her dad she was given two pennies. She also said, "When I went to church with Daddy, I knew before I got there that I wasn't supposed to like that piano."

One other issue with which Mack and Alma had to deal was Mack's medical practice and the strain that could and would put on their relationship. He talked with Alma when they were dating about what his life as a physician was like. He stood her up on a couple of dates because of patients he needed to see. They dated more often and more seriously as he began to establish his private medical practice. Mack asked Alma to think of all the reasons why they should not get married. Try as she could, Alma was unable to think of a single reason not to marry the handsomest man she had ever seen. She knew that she would play second fiddle to his work and she has, but she has been with him in every bit of his practice, supporting him with her prayers and her insomnia. One compensation Mack has offered her has been to give her everything he made treating patients on Sundays.

On October 4, 1940, they became engaged. Mack continues to remember that date and each year gives Alma a gift, like the two ceramic love birds he gave her in 1985, to commemorate the anniversary of their engagement. They did not tell their parents about their engagement because as Alma said, "It's nice to have a secret." About two months later they did tell Alma's parents about their plans to marry. But they did not tell Mack's parents until the night before their wedding.

It may be unusual during the last quarter of the twentieth century for a couple to go away from either one's home town to marry and to give such short notice to their parents, but this was common practice in the first half of the century. Mack and Alma did not elope because they announced their plans to their parents. When I asked them why they did not have a wedding in the church, Alma responded, "Only the aristocrats had church weddings in those days."

"And we didn't show in that ring," Mack chimed in immediately.

Marriage

With a light snow falling, Mack and Alma drove to Glasgow, Kentucky, on January 18, 1941, to be married. They drove to Burkesville, rode the ferry across the Cumberland River, arrived in Glasgow and were married around 8:00 p.m.

Motels were just beginning to be built, and while visiting a college classmate in Glasgow, Alma had seen the Windmills Motel in a romantic setting and had said, "There is where I want to spend my wedding night."

Mack was thirty-seven and Alma was twenty-three when they married. After spending their wedding night at the Windmills Motel, they spent the remainder of their honeymoon in Nashville, Tennessee. One place they visited was the Parthenon. While they were there, Mack looked the place over closely and concluded, "This would be a good place to hang tobacco, wouldn't it?" Alma tells this about Mack with a gleam in her eye and glee in her voice because, "He was witty and cute in a natural way."

When Mack and Alma returned to Monticello following their honeymoon, they moved into an apartment in the Hedrick Apartments. Alma worked as house keeper and in the summer canned vegetables to help with their winter food supply. Three daughters were born to them. Helen was born April 27, 1943, Ann was born January 31, 1945, and Marilyn was born April 16, 1947. Having three children born in four years caused Mack to quip, "If the youngins' keep coming this fast, we'll have to stop using double names."

Alma has been interested in every aspect of Mack's life. She has been with him in his practice and interested in similar hobbies like wildflowers and traveling. She also has been concerned about his appearance and the clothes that he wears.

Sometimes Mack would go to his office and ask if he were dressed okay. He said Alma had picked out his clothes and she had checked him over before he left home. After gaining people's approval that his clothes looked fine and matched just right, he would raise his pants legs to show that his socks didn't match. He deliberately mismatched his socks as a way to tease about Alma's insistence that his clothes match.

In a letter to me Mack wrote,

> I don't know if I made myself
> clear as to why I was attracted to

Alma as a wife. No. 1. She was a Christian. No. 2. She was an excellent conversationalist. No. 3. She was very beautiful. No. 4. She was extremely intelligent. After looking the field over for a few years I figured she was the one I wanted to be the mother of my three little girls, and do the cooking and housecleaning for the whole bunch of us.

    Many factors have contributed to Mack and Alma's marriage being meaningful, valuable, and lasting through more than forty-five years. They have been broadminded about each other, permitting each other to do things each wanted to do, encouraging each to support the church of his or her choosing both with presence and financial resources.

    Mack and Alma's family life has worked well also because Alma has been willing to keep things going at home when he was practicing medicine. Ask him what is the secret to his successful marriage, and he will respond, "We have a healthy respect for each other, and Alma has always been very broadminded."

    Strengths in their relationship from Alma's perspective include their religious beliefs, their strong devotion to God, and their commitment and devotion to each other. Qualities in Mack that have contributed positively to their marriage are his equanimity, his patience, his love for children, and his generous spirit. Alma said of Mack, "He has given me the moon." They both enjoy quoting from <u>Annabel Lee</u> by Edgar Allen Poe about the breadth and depth of their love for each other.

When Mack was a student at Cumberland College he did date one woman seriously. Nearly fifty years later when a drug salesman called on Mack and learned he had dated that particular Cumberland coed, the salesman promptly advised, "You should have married that woman!" Obviously, at the time the salesman offered his advice, he knew nothing of the delightful, romantic relationship Mack and Alma had shared for more than forty years.

Mack and Alma may not have shown in the aristocratic ring, but their marriage has shown well through the years. Their healthy respect and appreciation for each other have deepened their love and commitment to each other. These qualities have made their marriage both delightful and successful.

Mack and Alma Roberts

5
"I'VE HAD A LOT OF FUN"

Children have been of special interest in the Roberts family. Mack's affinity for children, his ability to relate comfortably to them, and his genuine enjoyment of children is a natural trait that he inherited from his father and grandfather. His love for children was illustrated personally for me when I called to tell him my children would like to meet him. With a loud, warm chuckle, he responded, "I think that would be wonderful!" He loves children, and they are naturally attracted to him, trusting him readily.

Mack's Dessert

Although Mack loves and relates well to all children, he does seem especially partial to girls. Sometime after his three daughters were born someone asked why he and Alma didn't have any boys. He promptly replied, "If we had wanted boys, we would have had boys."
He thoroughly enjoyed relating to his daughters as they grew up and continues to delight in them. When I asked his feelings about being the father of three daughters, a broad, warm, tender smile spread across his face as he said, "I've had a lot of fun."
When Alma became a mother she followed closely the model of her mother and accepted the primary responsibilty of child rearing because Mack was gone much of the time seeing patients. Alma's descriptive comment about that time was, "He had the dessert."

To enjoy his dessert and to give Alma a break from caring for three girls who were separated by only four years, Mack often would take the girls with him on house calls. He would leave his office over Rankin's Drugstore, drive to the house on North Main Street, pick up the girls in his four-wheel drive Jeep and head for some foreign part of Wayne County, foreign to the girls, but familiar to him. There is no part of Wayne County foreign to Mack. He has covered it all either by Jeep, by mule or on foot.

When the girls were with him and their journey led them to a creek, they would beg Mack to drive as fast as he could through the creek and make a big splash, which he would do. The splash would drown out the engine, Marilyn would be frightened and cry. Helen and Ann loved it because they could play in the creek while the water dried from the wires of the motor. This provided a good time, place, and the necessary cleaning material for Mack to change Marilyn's diaper. By the time this job was complete, all three girls were refreshed, they had had time to play, and the engine had dried off enough to start. They continued their journey to a patient's home.

Some of the roads Mack traveled were unbelievable and nearly impassible, only a four-wheel drive Jeep could make it. Helen recalls asking her dad once if the rutted and rocky road which they were bouncing over at about five miles per hour was the roughest road in the world. He said he guessed it was, and for a long time she felt a certain pride in having traveled such a distinguished route.

Many times Mack would have to park and walk a long distance, and when the girls were with him, he would leave them alone in the Jeep. Once as Mack was leaving the girls, he told them he was going to see a man who had been shot and the assailant had not be caught, so, "Lock the doors." Naturally, the girls´ imaginations went wild as they waited for their daddy to return. When he returned to the Jeep, they had the doors locked, had found some rope in the Jeep, tied and tangled the rope around the door handles in such a fashion they barely were able to get the rope loose for Mack to get in the Jeep. Luckily, the assailant hadn´t found the girls, and Mack was greatly amused at their efforts to keep the would be assailant out of the Jeep.

The girls never went into the house of a patient with their dad but remained in the Jeep observing the inevitable dog who came out to investigate them, the chickens, and other farm animals that might be near the house. Then Mack would emerge from the house, usually accompanied by a husband or wife or parent thanking him for having come. His invariable response was, "Let me know if he doesn´t get better." Sometimes he would tell the girls when he returned to the Jeep that the house did not have electricity. On the way home he would often point out the houses of other patients, reminding his daughters of previous trips they had made with him, or recalling having spent the night in a particular house while waiting for a baby to come.

When taking his dessert on these jaunts, Mack never seemed to be at a loss for entertainment. Often he would amuse the girls by singing hymns, but not in the ordinary way. He would sing in disguised voices and have the girls guess who he was imitating. They had at least two notorious singers in their family, an aunt known for her "country alto" and an uncle well-known for his high tenor vocal quality. This game was both amusing and entertaining to the girls because their dad did an excellent job of imitating the voices of these two relatives.

Rain often accompanied Mack and the girls when they went on house calls. While rain could dampen a trip and make the journey dreary, Mack would never let that happen. He invented a game whose object was to determine who could see the first raindrop hit the windshield. Mack won every time!

Back at home Mack kept his creative activities going as he related to the girls. A favorite snack was mayonnaise sandwiches. Mack would fix their sandwiches, they would sit down together to eat, and then he would have them pretend they were eating possum or bear.

When Mack went home for lunch or was home in the evening between house calls, his favorite place of rest was in the middle of the floor. But his being in the middle of the floor was too inviting to be resisted by the girls. They enjoyed playing on his back and giving him an "adjustment" by walking on his back. He would attempt to guess who was walking. Helen would be identified as Clint Green, a tall, slender man. Ann, who was a bit chubby at the time, would be referred to as Ed Brown, a rather rotund man who lived in Monticello. Ann did not mind the reference made by her dad, but she did not appreciate the giggling responses of her sisters.

As the girls grew older, they became more astute about their dad's invitations to travel with him on house calls. When he would call to ask if they would like to go with him, they began to investigate the situation by asking where he was going, how long he would be gone, but their most insightful question was, "Is this a granny case?" being interpreted, "Was he going to deliver a baby?" If the answer were, "Yes," the girls would decline the invitation because granny cases usually took an unpredictably long time.

Ponies For Sale? Never!

As the girls grew older they and their dad developed an interest in ponies. Actually, Mack asked them if they would prefer to have a bicycle or a pony for Christmas. The three girls discussed it and decided they preferred the pony. Mack already had asked Carl Rankin, who operated the drugstore beneath his office, to order him a bicycle for the girls. The net gain for them was a bicycle and a pony.

Helen, Ann, and Marilyn spent a tremendous amount of time with their ponies, petting, brushing, and riding them. The first pony was named Topper, and Mack bought a buggy for Topper to pull. He enjoyed watching the girls ride in the buggy with Topper harnassed to it. Although riding was fun, the girls preferred petting and talking to the ponies to riding them. Nobody knows all that the ponies heard from those three girls' mouths, but the ponies made excellent therapists. There were times when each girl was convinced that no one understood her like a pony did.

Soon after Topper came on the scene, it became evident, at least to Carl Rankin, that she was lonely. Carl gave the girls a goat to keep Topper company and Mack named the goat Carlotta. Getting a goat to serve as Topper's companion was a nice gesture, but apparently not to Topper's liking because she kept Carlotta corralled in one corner of the field day and night. Eventually, to be humane to Carlotta, the goat was returned to Carl. Topper was three years old when she became the first of the Roberts herd. She remained special to the girls until her death fifteen years later.

Because everyone, meaning Helen, Ann, Marilyn, and Mack, was convinced that Topper was lonely and Carlotta had not been the solution, the search was on for another pony or two. The Stardust Drive-In Theatre had four for sale and Mack bought them. Then on a trip to Barbourville he purchased seven more. These seven cost him $3,000. It seemed that in no time Mack and the girls were in the pony business full swing.

Naming the ponies was important and would not have been nearly as enjoyable without Mack's input. He came up with such innovative pony names as Penelope, Pegasus, Caesar, Piccolo Pete, Cindy Jane, and Hortense. During the year that My My won the Kentucky Derby, one of the Roberts' ponies had been bred to Mighty Sun, a Tennessee Walking Horse. The pony gave birth to a foal whose head was terribly disfigured. Mack named the colt, Oh My Goodness, and then always referred to it as Oh My.

The pony herd grew in numbers to thirty-five and eventually reached a maximum of fifty-one. Apparently Mack loved the ponies as much the girls did. At least they were convinced that he did. When anyone would asked to buy one of the ponies, he would say he had to talk it over with the girls. They would plead with him in tears not to sell a single one, and he didn't. Of course that necessitated buying winter feed for fifty-one ponies, but the girls didn't think of that, and Mack never showed any concern about it either. There were heartaches when a pony was sick, and when a colt or favorite pony died. Naturally, the girls cried. Mack didn't say much but seemed to empathize with them in their sadness. During times like these Mrs. Fronia Rankin, who lived across the street, would philosophize, "Them that has, lose."

Alma was the only member of the family interested in reducing the size of the pony herd. She would make her suggestion as winter was coming on or if one of the girls got injured some way working with the ponies. Alma was convinced that the ponies caused more heartache than pleasure, but Mack seemed always to side with the girls.

Ann was the victim of two serious accidents on Stardust, one of her favorite ponies. Once she fell off, broke her collarbone, and was unconscious for awhile. Her first words upon regaining consciousness were, "Daddy, don't sell the ponies!" The girls were convinced that he would never sell them while they were still at home, and he didn't.

One highlight of family life was the pony moving day which occurred twice each year. The ponies wintered about a mile away from the house on creek property that Mack owned. Each spring the ponies were walked from the creek to the maternity lot next to the house on North Main Street. Then in the Fall the ponies were taken back to the creek property to stay for the winter where there was a barn to protect them from the weather and to keep their feed dry.

When the time came to be divested of all ponies, only after the girls were grown and on their own, their value had diminished greatly. Mack sold forty ponies to one buyer, including the seven mentioned earlier, for $2,500. (This may have been the only business deal where Mack lost money.) Who got the most enjoyment from the ponies is a tossup, the girls riding them and spending time with them or Mack enjoying the girls enjoying the ponies.

You Are Special

Mack has been a family oriented person throughout his life. When his parents were living, Mack spent every Sunday afternoon visiting with them. Alma would do the same with her parents and the girls usually would alternate between the Roberts and Dolen grandparents. The Roberts family had a great sense of humor, and there was always lots of giggling going on which caused the girls to identify what is known to them as "the Roberts giggle." Some descendants had a stronger dose of it than others. Mack and Ottis in particular could really get the giggles going when they were together, especially in reminiscing about their childhood.

When Hobart, Mack's oldest brother, was alive, Mack often would take the girls by Hobart's feed store, usually on their way to or from a house call, where they would be told a few jokes and given a chunk of salt. Hobart would get out his pocket knife and knock off a chunk of cow salt for the girls to eat. The red block was far better than the yellow or the white!

Helen, Ann, and Marilyn uneqivocably state that their family life developed in a harmonious atmosphere. Their parents never argued about little things such as who takes out the garbage. They did argue on occasion about politics and religion. The girls did not learn what nagging or sulking meant until they got older and were away from home. In those formative years they just thought every family was like theirs.

Although the family never wanted for anything, they did live frugally. The girls were not spoiled in the sense of having many things, but Mack and Alma Roberts gave their daughters the gift of love. Each girl is convinced there was nothing her parents would not have done for her benefit. If they were spoiled, it was in their ability to have their parents' attention upon request. When one was homesick at college, they didn't tell her to tough it out, but, if she requested it, dropped everything and came to see her. Other times affectionate notes were sent regularly to the one needing some special attention.

Marilyn had a really difficult struggle with homesickness when she went to college. She got many notes from her dad, most of them were written on prescription blanks. Some of the more memorable prescriptions that he wrote Marilyn to help her survive homesickness were, "Call me every week," "Send gas money," "Send spending money," or there would be a picture of Prince and Dishman, her favorite horse and the man who cared for him. Evidence abounds that the girls were secure in knowing they were loved.

Mack was concerned each year that his daughters get the "right" teachers in school. For example, when Ann was in the fifth grade, she was placed in Mrs. Jennie Elam's class. Mrs. Elam was one of Mack's former teachers. Apparently, she really had been a tough teacher when he had her, and she still had that reputation in the hallways of the school. He was concerned that Ann would be in Mrs. Elam's class for an entire year. Either she had mellowed a bit through the years, or Ann was just sturdier than she or her dad expected, because she had a great and memorable year of school in Mrs. Elam's class.

Helen was a bookworm who thoroughly enjoyed reading. But occasionally Mack would tell her to close the book and go outside. He enjoyed seeing the girls play outside, and although he was eager for them to learn, he never believed that the only laboratory for learning was between the covers of a book. He never put pressure on the girls to achieve in school. They seemed to feel they received their share of that from their mother. Mack was always proud of the good grades that Helen, Ann, and Marilyn made, bragging in particular to Dr. William Tuttle with whom he shared office space.

Mack uniquely encouraged his daughters in their school work. All three girls were achievement oriented from the early days of their lives. Each in her own way seemed to desire the success and approval that came with achievement and giving her best effort. But their dad was known at times to give the girls money (a small amount), not for good grades but to salve their disappointment over bad ones.

The girls rarely if ever received a spanking from their dad and remember being corrected by him only a few times. Alma's comment to this situation is that she was the disciplinarian in the family because Mack wasn't there to do it. When the family bought their first television, there were some times when Mack thought the girls were watching too much of it, and he would send them to the garden to hoe the weeds out of the corn or beans. Other than a situation or two like this, Alma took responsibility for correcting and disciplining the girls.

Religious training was important in rearing their children and even though Mack and Alma did not attend the same church, their religious values were the same. Mack had strong feelings against smoking, consuming alcohol, and divorce. Warning against cheating in school was also a favorite theme.

The girls had jobs to do, especially in the summer, such as assisting with the laundry and house cleaning. They also washed the cars and were paid for this chore, saving the money in a travel fund for vacation. This work expectation continued throughout their development and their completion of college. Soon after Ann graduated from pharmacy school she was talking with Mack and said, "Daddy, I really don't enjoy working." And Mack replied, "What do you mean? After all I have spent for your education and you don't want to work!" The fact he said what he did and the tone with which he spoke caused Ann to reconsider how much she valued and enjoyed working.

An outstanding characteristic of Mack's parenting endeavors was that he was always interested in what his daughters were engaged in at school. This was demonstated in 1959 when Monticello High School went to the state torunament in basketball. He took a few days off from work and took the family to Louisville to follow the tournament play of the Trojans. Few parents did that with their children, unless they had a son on the squad.

Mack's interest and ability to relate to his daughters individually was evident in the baseball interest he shared with Ann. She was an avid New York Yankee and Mickey Mantle fan. For a few years, she lived and breathed it. Many mornings, Mack would wake Ann up by saying, "Mickey was 3 for 4 with a home run and 4 RBI's," or "Mantle hit 3 and Maris hit 2." This got Ann's day off to a great start, and her dad obviously sensed that. He saw her interest in baseball as a healthy one and he promoted it and shared it with her.

Through his attitude, actions, humorous comments, and warm affection, Mack has communicated to each of his daughters, "You are special. You're the only one of your kind." Helen is special because she is the first born. Ann feels special because she is the middle one and people often commented about Ann to Mack, "Oh, she looks just like you." Marilyn was special because she was the baby. Ann said it was fun to walk down the street with her dad because people would stop him and talk to him and then talk to her. The feeling of specialness cannot be pretended. Either it is authentic or it isn't. The specialness of Mack's daughters to him is clear and unquestioned by him and them.

Twenty-Five Cents to Peek, Fifty Cents To Hold

Mack and Alma's interest and support of their daughters did not end when the the girls were grown. Many examples of the specialness of their daughters are revealed through their continued involvement with the girls and their families.

After arriving home with Tara, her first baby, Ann, exasperated, called her parents to ask, "How do you put her down?" Alma had a terrible cold, but she and Mack drove to Paris, Tennessee to lay down their granddaughter and to calm her mother and father.

When Tara made her first visit to see her grandparents in Monticello, Granddaddy put a sign on the bedroom door where Tara was, "Twenty-five cents to peek, fifty cents to hold." When lying on the floor with Tara a few months later, he was overheard telling her, "We're going to send you to the University of Vienna" (pronounced Vī·ē·na by him, as in Viena sausage).

Mack enjoyed going around with Helen and Pat when they were looking for a house in Cookville, Tennessee. After seeing the first one he commented, "I like this one best." The house they eventually bought had a small kitchen. Helen is an excellent cook and entertains some, but she is not known as one who spends an excessive amount of time in the kitchen. However, Helen was sure that her dad would think the kitchen was too small. She said something to him about the small kitchen when he came for a visit to which he responded, "I think it's big enough for you."

Tara severly cut her right check at age two, resulting in a scar, and several years later a cut on her chin required stitches. When the time came to remove the stitches, Tara called Granddaddy and asked him to come to Tennessee to do the job. He went to Tennessee. Tara had a doll named Mrs. Beasley that Mack sewed up and removed the stitches to show Tara how it would be done. They went to see the doctor who had sewn up Tara's cut. Ann remarked, "He was at least twenty-five years younger than Daddy. It was obvious that his hands were shaking. Daddy's hands were as calm as could be." Granddaddy removed Tara's stitches for her.

Mack enjoys each of his grandchildren, entertaining them with the Jew's harp, repeating with them many of the games, stories, and humor he had shared with his children. When little Mack , the youngest grandchild, was enrolled in a preschool class, his turn to bring refreshments came. Granddaddy volunteered to prepare the refreshments for the class. He made apple puzzles for each member of the class. He knows how to cut an apple in configurations so the apple will remain intact as a whole but can be taken apart and put together as a puzzle. When the fascination with the puzzle has ended, the apple tastes better. A mother of one preschooler said Dr. Roberts made life rough for all the other parents who prepared refresments. Their cookies and punch never measured up to the apple puzzles that Mack Drake had brought to school!

Mack's grandchildren said that he always keeps things even on birthdays. The birthday person receives $10 and each of the others receives $5. This way no one feels left out; yet, the one with the birthday is treated in a more special way that day.

In earlier years he would divide with the grandchildren any payment he received from house calls when they were visiting with him, but he had to make new arrangements after Mack Drake was born because he lived next door. Otherwise the Kentucky grandchild would have an advantage over the Tennessee grandchildren, and that would be unfair. The one situation where Mack wants Kentucky having an advantage over Tennessee is in basketball.

Mack has communicated specialness to his grandchildren like he did to his daughters. Tara thinks she is special to Granddaddy because she is the first grandchild. Mark considers himself to be special because he is the first grandson. Aimee identifies her personality as the trait that makes her special to Granddaddy, commenting, "He doesn't like a grump." Aimee is able to size up a situation well. It is this quality which has caused Mack to respond, "I'm putting my money on Aimee Doodle."

Mark said if you see something you like, Granddaddy will get it for you. He saw a cow he liked and the next Christmas there was a note in his stocking that Granddaddy was having the cow shipped to Tennessee for Mark. Then to keep things even, as he seems determined to do, he later gave Tara and Aimee each a cow. Mack Drake, the youngest grandchild is special because he lives next door to Poppie and because he is named Mack. Surely the greatest gifts that can be given to children is for them to know they are loved and special to someone. Mack Roberts has given these gifts readily and unequivocally to his children and his grandchildren.

Traveling

Mack loves to travel whether he is going to Hidalgo or Heidleburg. His interest in traveling, unrelated to work, developed suddenly in the late 1940´s. His medical practice had caused him to be on call twenty-four hours a day, seven days a week. He had never taken a vacation or given any thought to taking one. He was reading an article in a medical journal, "H Stands For Heart Disease." The article was about a country doctor who had worked like Mack was working and his will was being probated because he had died of a heart attack. Mack was forty-four and had never had a vacation. He went home and announced to Alma, "Get your youngins´ together. We´re going to Florida." They took two weeks to go to Florida, and he has taken at least two weeks for vacation every year since then. Alma thoroughly enjoyed vacations once they started taking them because, "Tonight I have him all to myself. No one will call him tonight." Of course that also meant she would get an uninterrupted night of sleep.

Vacations also were the only times that the family was able to eat meals uninterrupted by patients either calling on the telephone or coming to the house for Mack to see them. Mack said that whenever he went on vacation he always made somebody mad. Babies are due all along and it is impossible to take vacation only after all the babies are born.

The family went to Florida for several consecutive years and drove across the United States one summer. Later they took a three week trip to the Northwest, and then one to New England. They saw all the sights, and Mack was definitely intent that the girls were interested in it all, reminding them that he didn´t get out of Wayne County until he was sixteen years old. At lookout points in the Smokies and the Grand Canyon, if the girls didn't hop out of the car to look, they were immediately urged to do so.

Mack and Alma have been abroad to visit Europe and Asia. He was in his late sixties before his first experience on a plane, a transatlantic flight. Since then he has flown many times, always with a great sense of awe; he often says that he wishes he could call up Christopher Columbus and take him with him on a 747 transoceanic flight. What took Columbus sixty-six days took Mack six hours. He is a good traveler, always flexible, always interested in and inquisitive about the sights and cultures of other regions.

Mack and Alma treated Ann to a Scandinavian trip with them to give her a break from her three children who were six, five, and three at the time. He has enjoyed every trip and is ready to go again immediately after completing a trip. Those who travel with him always need a lot more time to recuperate from the trip than he does. One day he entered a grocery store in Monticello where his nephew was working. Mack was wearing a bright, plaid hat. Milton commented on his hat and Mack responded, "Got that in Ireland. Dudn't fit just right. Might take it back." He may take it back yet!

Extended Family

Two of Mack's close friends, Bill Tuttle and Carl Rankin, were like members of the family because of their close association with Alma and the girls as well as with Mack. Bill Tuttle was a third generation dentist in Monticello, and he and Mack shared office space in the Rankin building for thirty-two years and then moved together into a new building in 1971. They shared that office building until Bill's death in 1983. Bill and Mack really liked and respected each other. Both were easy going and enjoyed teasing one another.

Tuttle, as Mack affectionately referred to him, constantly was warning Mack against permitting his children to have candy or soft drinks. Whenever the girls were at the office Mack always would find an opportune time to sneak them downstairs to the drugstore to buy them a cherry coke. This may have been as much to aggravate Tuttle as it was to please the girls. After Mack's seventy-fifth birthday he gloated in waving his social security check in front of Tuttle several times each month before cashing it.

Nobody can remember a time when Tuttle and Mack had a disagreement. They enjoyed their daily contact with each other and delighted in swapping stories about patients. Mack never missed an opportunity to urge Tuttle to quit smoking. Tuttle kept on smoking, and Mack kept on urging.

During Bill's illness, he was able to stay at home as he wanted because Mack went by to see him at least once each day. Mack was really upset when Tuttle died. No doubt he felt deeply that a significant part of himself had died. Mack and Tuttle were warm, genuine friends.

Carl Rankin owned and operated the drugstore on the first floor of the building where Mack's office was. They visited with each other every day. Mack and Carl seemed to have a similar sense of humor and the same interests—medicine, and the bank where both were members of the Board of Directors.

Carl also was close to the family and took a great interest in the girls. He always wanted to see their report cards, knew their ponies' names, gave them special gifts at Christmas that included dolls, electric trains, and chemistry sets.

Mack and Carl took a great interest in Edison Dishman, a constant inhabitant of the city jail because of an alcohol problem. They would bail him out of jail, take him to one of their gardens to work, and eventually succeeded in curing him of his alcoholism. Dishman, as he became known affectionately, was a long-time friend and extended family member. He became the chief pony caretaker, counting and checking them daily in exchange for the rental payment on a house that Mack owned.

In 1959 Carl Rankin suffered a cerebral hemmorhage. During the days that Carl was hanging on to life, Mack became the most withdrawn and quiet any of the family had ever seen him. All Mack could say at that time about Carl was, "He's about as low as he can be." Carl died in a few days and it was a devastating loss to the entire family, but especially to Mack.

Characteristics

Patience and fairness are two characteristics that permeate Mack's personality. Family, friends, and patients have observed these qualities in him and commented about their contribution to Mack's relationships with people.

Patience

The only indicator anyone has noticed which hints that Mack is troubled, uneasy, or uncomfortable about a situation is when he hums. In tense situations, his humming is a clue that he is feeling a bit uneasy. Two recurring situations that have given rise to Mack's humming his way to easiness are when he is attempting to end an argument or when he has to go into a motel office to rent a room. Mack is a shy man, especially beyond Wayne County, but his patience and easy going nature seem always to prevail. Patience, confidence, and optimism are interrelated qualities that enable Mack to take the long view of a situation. He often adds a bit of humor that keeps things in perspective. There was concern when Marilyn was a child that she was too dependent on taking a bottle. She was still taking a bottle before her afternoon nap when she was five years old. Her dad's comment was, "Maybe by the time she courts the boys, she'll quit the bottle." As far as I have been able to determine, his prophecy was fulfilled. Regardless of the situation or circumstance, Mack doesn't panic, and when people are in his presence, they don't panic either.

An example of Mack's calm, assuring manner occurred when he was asked his opinion when Marilyn was about to marry. "If it suits her, it suits me."

He is the ultimate optimist in many respects. He is convinced that events will work out well. Mack's grandson, Mack Drake, was born two months prematurely and nearly died his first night. The next morning the baby had stablized, Mack went in to visit Marilyn and calmly commented, "Well things turned out pretty well, didn't they?" There was something about his manner and tone that conveyed confidence and optimism which Marilyn and Rick experienced as extremely comforting.

The only time family members have seen Mack impatient is when they were trying to leave town on a trip. Then he is in a hurry because he loves to take trips, and he doesn't want a patient to catch him, causing him to delay or postpone the trip. It has happened times too numerous to count.

Although nothing ruffles him, there was one occasion when Mack became extremely upset. He was prepared to take some pictures of the Great Stone Faces in North Dakota and his camera didn't work. No one, including Mack, knows why that upset him so much, except that he had paid "good" money for that camera and he expected it to work.

Fairness

He does not like to be cheated. The best illustration of this is the clock he purchased in Switzerland. When he got it home, it didn't work. A couple of years later he was taking another trip to Switzerland and he took the clock with him. The store clerk claimed he couldn't have bought the clock there because they didn't sell that brand. Mack asked to talk with the manager. Although he was gone for the day, he learned that the manager would be in the next day. He browsed around the shop for a few minutes and located the brand of his clock on the shelf. The next day Mack returned to the shop, caught the manager there, and exchanged his clock for one that worked properly.

Bargaining

Mack's patience and fairness are blended in the delightful pleasure of bargaining. He enjoys persuading someone to reduce the price on an item he is interested in buying. While on the Scandinavian trip mentioned previously, he, Alma, and Ann went shopping one day in different directions. When they got back together, Mack and Ann each had bought identical items. Mack wanted to know how much Ann had paid for hers. She had

paid the asking price. He had gotten his for a dollar cheaper.
    Helen enjoyed the time her dad was with her when she was buying shrubs for her yard. Mack had a great time dealing with the nursery owner and asking him what the price of the shrubs were if they bought two or three or a dozen. When they got ready to leave, he instructed the man to put the plants in the Cadillac out there to which the man responded, "Now I know why you´re driving a Cadillac."

Hobbies

    A contributing factor to Mack´s enjoyment of life has been the variety of interests and hobbies he has developed and maintained throughout his life. He loves the outdoors, including gardening, although when he would get his garden clothes on and crank up his tiller, a patient would interrupt him. Yet, that never seemed to upset him. Maintaining varied interests but never being consumed by them has contributed to Mack´s well-rounded life.

Collectibles

    He thoroughly enjoys driving through the countryside, observing nature as he goes, identifying the trees and wildflowers as he drives along the rough country roads making house calls. He often marks a young tree or a clump of wildflowers, takes a shovel with him the next time he travels to that section of the county, digs up the tree or flowers and transplants them in his yard. The hillside behind his house is covered with wildflowers, many of which he has transplanted in this fashion. He pointed out an Indian Paint Brush to me as we rode along, but admitted that it didn't grow well in captivity. He also enjoys spring bulbs and delights in keeping his daughters supplied with them. What he enjoys and what beautifies his yard, he wants his daughters to enjoy in their yards.

Mack also delights in beautiful china and dainty figurines; if given a choice in a large department store, he will always head for the china department. For his eighty-second birthday his family gave him a set of china he had admired; and, not to be outdone, he reciprocated by surprising each of his daughters with a lovely set at each of their birthdays.

Mack is fascinated with exotic birds, like frizzy chickens that look like they have been put through a stove pipe backwards. He has peacocks in the barn on the property where he lives. Alma said that he should be ashamed keeping them in the barn, to which Mack responded, "It's their own fault. The doors are open, but they won't come out."

He bought two roosters and two hens for his grandson, Mark, when Mark was five. Mark was delighted to have them and when his parents took him to the farm to see them, Mark ran out to where the chickens were. It was summer and Mark was wearing shorts but no shirt. One rooster flogged Mark and scratched his back badly. That was a frightening experience for Mark, and the caretaker of the farm refused to feed that rooster saying, "I don't feed anything that fights me."

A varied menagerie of birds (as well as squirrels and chipmunks) takes advantage of Mack's well-stocked bird feeders the year round. Humming birds are special favorites, and sitting in the breakfast nook, he enjoys pointing out the window to one feeding on the deck railing.

Pat, Mack's first son-in-law, recalls having gone with Mack on a house call not long after he and Helen had married. Not knowing his father-in-law well, Pat was casting about for some topic of conversation, noted a covey of doves which flew up beside the road. "What's the limit on doves in Kentucky?" Pat asked. "None, as far as I am concerned," was Mack's instant reply.

Mack is a collector. He has collected carved ivory from Hong Kong, a vase from England, a cabinet from Rome, a bust from Egypt, wildflowers from Slickford, and arrowheads from Gap Creek. Once he saw some arrowheads on boards at the Wayne County Armory that were to be sold at auction that night. He contacted Glenn Denny and asked him to bid them off for him. Glenn told him they would probably be expensive. Mack said, "Just buy 'em and bring them to me. I'll be up." Glenn was concerned about spending someone else's money and he asked Mack what was the limit he wanted to spend. Mack said, "Just buy 'em." Glenn bought two boards of arrowheads for $100 each. Later Marilyn had them put into walnut frames and they hang in his office at his house.

Love For The Farm

Because farming is in his blood, Mack has enjoyed buying some small farms over the years. He claimed the main reason he bought the properties was for the tobacco base on each of them. Mack strongly opposes people using tobacco because he thinks it is bad for their health. When asked if he saw any inconsistency in his opposition to people using tobacco and his buying land to have more tobacco base for raising and selling tobacco, he said, "Yeah, there is inconsistency there. But it's hard for my tenant to make a living without raising and selling tobacco."

One piece of property he bought was on Coal Bank Mountain. He bought a hundred acres for $1,000. Later, coal was discovered on it and three acres of it were mined for coal. He sold $26,000 worth of coal off the three acres. He sold the timber off the 100 acres for $1,500 and he still owns the property. He owns 434 acres in Wayne County and 100 acres in McCreary County.

Hunting

Shooting his twenty-two rifle is one of Mack's pleasures. He used to keep it in his Jeep to have it with him when he was in the country making house calls. That way he was prepared to shoot ducks, squirrels, and rabbits to put meat on the table, which he did several times. Grandson Mark was impressed that at age 82 his grandfather could take his twenty-two scopeless rifle and shoot a lizard sunning on a rock thirty feet away. Mack hasn't lost his childhood enjoyment for hunting.

"I Slept With Elmer Brammer"

Being a staunch Republican has made politics a perennial interest for Mack. In the 1940's he campaigned for Republican candidates. His brother, Hobart, served one term as county judge. His nephew, Milton Roberts, served one term as County Court Clerk.

During the 1945 election campaign Mack served as the unofficial treasurer for the Republican Party. In those days one operation of party politics was to pay people to go to the polls to vote. This was not interpreted or understood as buying votes because you couldn't make a person vote a certain way or check up to see how he voted. There were people in one's own party who would not vote unless they got something for their trouble of going to the polls. Money was collected to be used on election day. During this campaign, as well as others, the Republicans didn't want the Democrats to know how much election day money they had. Several different people got five dollar bills from the bank to donate to the Election Day Kitty. They paid people to participate in the election and $5 was the going rate. They also paid people gas money to use their cars as taxis to get people to the polls. The pollster taxi drivers were paid when the polls closed. Mack served as the keeper of the Kitty. He kept about $10,000 in a shoe box for two weeks before the election. Whenever he left the office to make a call, he carried his medical bag in his hand with the shoe box tucked under his arm.

As he and I were riding up the valley near Coal Bank Mountain, he pointed to a house on the hillside and said, "I slept with Elmer Brammer right there! He was running for tax commissioner. We were out here campaigning and it got to be late so we spent the night there." The glee in his voice clearly communicated he enjoyed being involved in county politics.

Gospel Music

Mack has always enjoyed listening to and singing gospel music. Two of his favorite groups that he listens to on Sunday mornings are the Chuck Wagon Gang and the Spear Family. George Beverly Shea and Tennessee Ernie Ford are his favorite vocalists. His enjoyment not only is in listening, but also singing along, or at least humming. This is part of the way that he prepares himself for worship on Sundays.

Banking

A long time and long term interest of Mack has been the Monticello Banking Company where he has been a stockholder since 1948 and bank President since 1978. When the bank directors were deciding on a new President, Dr. Roberts spoke to Charles Cowan urging him to be the Chairman of the Board. Charles suggested Dr. Roberts be Chairman, to which Dr. Roberts responsed, "Nope. You be Chairman and I´ll be President. There´s more prestige in being President."

He began his investment in the Monticello Banking Company in 1948. Tom Ragan owned 150 shares of bank stock and he became upset because the bank directors had decided to hire a manager, James Lee McNeely, from outside Wayne County. Tom felt strongly that they did not need any foreigner in there to operate the bank. Because this decision had been made, Tom wanted to sever his relationship with the bank.

Tom decided to sell his bank stock, and he wanted $200 per share for his 150 shares. One person contacted Mack about buying half of Tom´s shares and then Tom contacted Mack about buying all the shares. Mack said he did not have that much money, $30,000. Tom told him he could pay him for the stock as he had some money available and that he could pay whatever interest rate he wanted. Mack accepted these arrangements and decided to pay 4% interest. Loans were being made then at 5% and 6% interest. No written agreement or contract was signed. The two men made a verbal agreement on their business transaction. Whenever Mack accumulated a little money he would make a payment to Tom until he finally paid off the debt. Later the stock split two shares for each share owned and still later the stock split six shares for each share owned. The 150 shares eventually became 1,800 shares. The book value on the stock in 1986 was $350 to $400 per share. Mack continues his interest in the bank and enjoys serving in the prestigious position of President.

"From Beginning to End"

I asked Dr. Roberts what had been the most fun thing about life for him and he said, "From the beginning to the end." Of course the end hasn't come for him yet, but this was his way of saying that life had been delightful for him up to the present moment. The truth of this statement seems clearest in his relationships with Alma, his daughters, his sons-in-law, and his grandchildren. He has had a lot of fun throughout his life and his involvement with his family and friends bears witness that Mack Roberts enjoys living.

Mack, Helen, Ann, and Marilyn on their first Florida vacation.

Mack and his first grandchild, Tara.

Alma and Mack sightseeing in Greece.

Pat and Helen Deese.

Bill, Ann, Aimee, Tara, and Mark Looney.

Mack, Marilyn, and Rick Drake.

Dr. Roberts, Otis Eads, and Charles Cowan receiving an award for the Monticello Banking Company from a representative of Kentucky Educational Television.

6

"I'VE LOVED EVERY MINUTE OF IT"

Dr. Roberts defines being a physician as a vocation in the classical meaning of vocation. Vocation means calling, and suggests that a person is led or drawn into one's life work because of the meaning and importance of the task and the conviction that he has the skills and interest to contribute significantly to the betterment of human beings through this calling.

A vocation is different from a profession. A profession is how a person earns a living and may be the only reason for doing a certain task, to make a living. A vocation is a calling to dedicate one's life to a particular type of work to benefit the lives of others. In a vocation the primary concern is the use of one's abilities for the benefit of other people. In a profession the primary emphasis is on earning an income.

Dr. Roberts considers his vocation a part of his stewardship of the gift of life that God has given him. "God gave me the ability to be a doctor, and I think I ought to use that ability as long as I'm able," expresses his deep conviction. Alma's obervation about his vocational attitude bears out this same view. She said if she were writing this book she would title it "A Living Sacrifice" because he has given himself sacrificially to his fellow human beings.

Dr. O. M. Carter influenced Dr. Roberts to consider becoming a physician. Most people are influenced by people in a particular vocation to enter that field of work. In an earlier era the custom was for a doctor to groom someone to take his place or to encourage young people to consider entering the medical field and then return to their home towns to help with the health care of the citizens. This was part of the process of receiving a calling or entering a vocation.

Following medical school Dr. Roberts wanted to do an internship at St. Joseph's Hospital in Lexington, but his indebtedness was so great that he needed a job to pay off his student incurred debts. Wayne County was searching for a Health Officer, and Dr. Roberts was given the job earning $216 per month. His reaction to that salary was, "I thought I was half rich."

During the first six months of this job, Dr. Roberts didn't have a car but the County Health Nurse, Edna Brooking, did. They worked out an agreement for their travels to the schools and communities where they went to provide health and medical care. She provided the car and Dr. Roberts bought the gas. When the schools were in session, the County Health Office staff would travel to the schools and give children vaccinations for smallpox and typhoid. This was the first meeting many children had with a doctor.

He served as Health Officer for five years. During that time he lived with his parents in Oil Valley, traveling to and from Monticello each day. For the first few months he either caught a ride with someone or used a horse and buggy. After about six months he was able to buy his first car, a second hand Model A Ford coupe for $125. It was a good car but the tires were old. He drove it to Sunnybrook over some fresh W. P. A. roads. When he returned to Monticello the tires were cut to pieces and he had to buy four new ones.

Aleta Roberts, one of Dr. Roberts' receptionists, remembers seeing him when she was a student at the Mill Springs School. As he got ready to give her her vaccination, he commented,

"Another tough hided Roberts." This humorous comment helped Aleta be more at ease in receiving her vaccination.

While serving as Health Officer, Dr. Roberts traveled to places in Wayne County about which he had heard but to which he had never been. This job enabled him to pay off his indebtedness and to learn his way around every hill, valley, and crevice of Wayne County.

As Health Officer, Dr. Roberts held a venereal disease clinic every Saturday morning. He held baby clinics, clinics for prospective mothers, and also had a clinic for the Wayne County midwives, of which there were several in those years.

Betty Tuttle, an employee in the Health Office, told about going with Dr. Roberts to visit a new mother who had just given birth to twins. It was a cold winter day with snow on the ground. Betty commented,

> I will never forget the meagerness of that family's existence. The mother was in a bed with barely enough covers to keep herself and the twins warm. There was practically no furniture, barren floors, and a poor fire in an old fireplace. Dr. Roberts returned to town and bought some much needed items and food for the mother and the twins to take back out to them. I am sure he did this at his own expense.[1]

Emergencies were part of Dr. Roberts' practice as County Health Officer. When the Ohio River flooded January 22-23, 1937, about one hundred refugees were bussed into Monticello and housed in the new city jail on Columbia Avenue. Some of the men had to occupy the jail cells and some families were bedded down on the upper floor where the City Police Judge held court.

One Louisville woman had two young sons and a pretty little daughter about three years old. Her sons got into a fight and one stabbed the other in the arm with a pocket knife. Dr. Roberts attended to his wound. The mother was ashamed of her sons and her distress and embarrassment were evident. After treating the boys, Dr. Roberts went to town and bought the little girl a pair of pretty white kid shoes, hoping to make the family feel better. All these refugees were from the poorest section of Louisville and had lost everything. Dr. Roberts vaccinated them for typhoid. It was difficult caring for so many people in such a small amount of space. The stench from the disinfectant being used only added to the emotional misery of the situation.

Dr. Roberts resigned his position as County Health Officer in the spring of 1938 to begin a year of internship at St. Joseph's Hospital on July 1. Dr. Roberts wanted the experience and training that an internship provided. He completed his internship on June 30, 1939 and returned to Monticello to open his private medical practice.

The Practice

In 1939, when Dr. Roberts began his private practice in Monticello, there were seven doctors practicing medicine in the county. They were O. M. Carter, Perry Parrigan, C. F. Holtegel, E. B. Rice, T. H. Gamblin, C. B. Rankin, and Frank Duncan. Dr. Roberts and Dr. Duncan were the young doctors in town.

Getting Started

Getting a medical practice underway was not an easy task. People already were established with a doctor, and they were not eager to change nor did they want to risk their care with the new doctor in town. Although it had been helpful that many people had met Dr. Roberts when he was the County Health Officer, they were reluctant to adopt him as their regular physician. It was slow getting patients to come to him. What he had to do was to take care of people who came to him for medical help. He operated on the premise that if he treated people, was fair with them, and made a good impression, they would call on him the next time. Gradually, he began to add a patient or two to his practice.

Driving over Edwards Mountain recently, Dr. Roberts pointed out a wide, flat place beside the road. He said he once drove to that spot in the snow and parked his car. A man met him with a red mule. Dr. Roberts rode the mule two miles to the man's house to treat a member of his family. "That was 1939. He paid me $10. I thought I was flying."

During the first two years when Dr. Roberts was establishing his practice, the older doctors began to retire or die. The result was that eventually he and Dr. Duncan were the only physicians providing health and medical care for the entire county.

By the end of the second year of Dr. Roberts' practice, the United States was thrust into World War II. Not long after the United States became involved in the war, Dr. Duncan entered military service and that left Dr. Roberts as the only doctor to serve Wayne County. He worked day and night seven days a week. That was a gruelling pace, and it is amazing he survived it without some long term negative effect on his own health.

When Dr. Roberts began his practice his fees were $1 for an office call, $2.50 for a house call in town and a dollar per mile beyond the city limits. He charged $25 for delivering a baby whether it took twenty minutes or two days, and $30 for delivering twins. Many times he did not receive the fee or received it in some barter form such as pies, cakes, or garden vegetables. One man gave him $5 and a bushel of apples which probably was worth two or three dollars at the time. Another man offered him two gallons of moonshine whiskey for delivering his baby, but Dr. Roberts refused. The authorities confiscated that man's still and arrested him in 1986, more than forty years later for making and selling moonshine. He had been at it a long time! Dr. Roberts regretted not accepting the moonshine to have as a souvenir.

Raymond Duncan said that Dr. Roberts delivered his first child and wrote, "Money was hard to come by back then, and I paid him $5 down and $5 a month until paid. He may have forgotten it, but I have not. I want to thank you Doc, again, forty years later."

Early in his practice Dr. Roberts was asked to make a house call to deliver a baby. The father told him in advance he didn't have the money, but he would give him two guinea hens for his services. Dr. Roberts agreed and went to the family's house, delivered the baby, and then had to go with the man to the chicken yard to help catch his guineas. Guineas are difficult to catch and these two, in their panic, tried to get away. One guinea impaled itself on the picket fence, and suddenly Dr. Roberts' earnings had been diminished by fifty percent.

On another occasion, after delivering the baby and waiting to receive his fee, the father said he didn't have the money because this situation "kind of slipped up on me." Dr. Roberts left with the man owing him the $25 fee. He has done that many times, often not receiving any payment or receiving partial or total payment later.

In August of 1975 Lizzie Jones went to Dr. Roberts' office to see him. Her reason for going was to pay him what she owed him. He looked up her records and could not find a bill. He asked her for what service she wanted to pay. She said, "I want to pay you for delivering that baby." Dr. Roberts scratched his head, looked puzzled, and asked when he had delivered her baby. She said, "Well, he was thirty-one years old this week." The woman was receiving monthly social security payments, and she paid the $25 which was the fee in 1944 when her son was born.

Dr. Roberts has learned from his patients that the universal pay day is Saturday. Often a patient will say, "Doc, I don't have the money right now, but I'll pay you Saturday."

"What they don't say is <u>which</u> Saturday they'll pay me."

Because of Dr. Roberts' patient, easy-going nature, people sometimes take advantage of him. Family and friends at times are convinced that patients take advantage of him all the time. But he is able to stand his ground with anyone and to determine when to be firm and when to be flexible. He received a call from a man in the middle of the night to come to his house to deliver a baby. It was the heart of the winter, the temperature was below zero, and snow and ice were on the ground. The family had not paid him for the previous two deliveries, and Dr. Roberts reminded the father of this on the telephone when he called for him to deliver number three. The man admitted his failure to pay, but said he had the $25 for this one. Dr. Roberts agreed to go. He rolled out into the cold night air and crept along the icy roads for several miles in his Jeep to the family's house. In a couple of hours he delivered the baby, cleaned up, put his hat and coat on, and the father gave him $10. Dr. Roberts took his hat off, hung it on the nail, sat down at the kitchen table, and said, "You told me you had the $25. I'm going to sit right here until you pay me." The man went into another room and returned with the additional $15.

I'm not sure we can appreciate what it is like to be awakened in the middle of the night, night after night, with someone wanting us to come to see him unless we have experienced this first hand. Dr. Roberts' daugther, Helen, has given an excellent personal description of what it was like for her to be awakened by those telephone calls, overhear her dad's side of the conversation, and then hear him head out into the cold darkness at 2:00 a.m.

> One vivid memory dominates my recollections of my father in his role as physician. It is a memory not of a single occurrence, but of a scene repeated almost nightly. In the middle of the night, the phone rings. It awakens me, and I lie still and listen to Daddy slowly getting out of bed in the next room and walking in the darkness to the phone in the wall. (Having more than one phone was unknown in those days, and ours was deliberately not located in the bedroom.) He finally stops the ring-

ing by picking up the receiver, and I listen to one side of the conversation; the certain inquiries: "Who did you say? Whose boy is he? When did he get sick?"

And, after this probing, always the capitulation: "I suppose I can get out there." Then I listen to him dress, open the basement door locking it behind him, and go down the steps. The doors of the basement garage are opened with a grating sound as they drag along the concrete floor. Then the sound of the Jeep starting. Lying warmly and sleepily in my bed I marvel as I marvel every time this happens that he can make himself get up and go out into the cold and darkness. As a child and even as a teenager I felt that I would never be strong enough to make myself do this. And so the often-repeated scene has remained to me an image of his dedication to his profession and to the people. I suppose there were greater sacrifices from his own point of view than getting out of a warm bed on a cold night, but to me in my childhood this was an ultimate one.[2]

Variations on this scene would occur when the family of the sick had no phone. The patient's pain or the fear of family members would cause a member of the patient's family to come to Dr. Roberts' house in the middle of the night. Once again Helen gives a descriptive account.

We had no doorbell, so the sound we woke up to was an alarming banging on the door, often accompanied by shouts for "Doc." This would be followed by the same slow movement of Daddy getting up and going through the darkness to the front door. He would turn on the porch light and open the door, exposing himself to the mercy of whoever was there, protected only by a screen door attached to the jamb by a latch. Sometimes the patient had been brought in, and Daddy would direct them down the driveway and into the basement. He would turn on the basement light for them, then put on his pants over his pajamas and go down. On other occasions the caller at the door would be there to plead the case of the patient who would be too ill to be brought in, and I would hear now both sides of the negotations. First the details of the sickness, the anxiety of the speaker apparent; then the directions to the house, frequently complicated, involving the houses of others more prominent or at least more prominently located on a road as a reference point. And in my childhood, the invariable question from my father: "Can you drive all the way?" Sometimes a quick affirmative in response, sometimes an apologetic but urgent "No, but we'll have a mule at the road waiting for you." Often this would be followed by an attempt at what a salesman of today would call "closure": "I've got the money, Doc."[3]

This nightly interruption of rest and sleep has had little adverse effect on Dr. Roberts. His ability to rest anywhere anytime has benefited his health and his disposition.

Dr. Roberts also is able to conserve his energy. An evening visitor in the Roberts home observed him conserving energy when a patient drove into the driveway. One of his daughters told him that it looked like a patient had pulled in the driveway. "Okay." He continued to visit with his guests. The patient went down to the basement where the doctor usually saw patients, but there were no lights turned on in the basement. In a few minutes the man came to the front door, pounded on the door, and Dr. Roberts went to the door.

"My wife is sick, Doc. I went down to the basement first."

"It's dark down there, isn't it?"

"Yeah."

"Take her down to the basement. I'll turn the light on and meet you down there."

Dr. Roberts did not get in a hurry, and he did not waste energy by rushing and then waiting for the patient. He was at ease waiting and when he was waiting, he was conserving his energy.

It was difficult for Dr. Roberts and his family to have privacy. Once when Dr. Roberts was seeing a patient in the basement and Alma was in the kitchen preparing supper, she heard the door close and thought he had come into the house. In a minute she was startled by the strange voice of a patient who was waiting for Dr. Roberts saying, "I just thought I'd come in and see what you were doing."

Because Dr. Roberts is a general practitioner of medicine he has done a little bit of everything: consultations with other physicians, internal medicine, orthopedics, obstetrics, pediatrics, and surgery. During the early years of his practice he performed tonsillectomies for $25. Three tonsillectomy patients were Alma and two daughters, but he didn't charge them. Theirs were family courtesy.

One of his patient's was born with two fingers on each hand grown together. This made it difficult for her to use her fingers. She wondered if Dr. Roberts could "cut her fingers apart." He thought he could and proceeded to do "plastic surgery" in his office. He separated the fingers on one hand, then he had to split the skin on each of the fingers to have enough skin to sew up each finger. He completed the procedure. It was successful and he charged her $10, but he never got around to operating on the fingers on the woman's left hand.

Through the years of his practice, Dr. Roberts has delivered over 4,400 babies, including two of his own and this writer. More than 4,000 of these babies were delivered in homes, and he delivered at least one in the patient's car in his driveway on North Main Street.

His fees really have not increased in proportion to the cost of other things during the past fifty years. Dr. Roberts' fees in 1986 were $10 for an office visit and $15 for a house call. If the house call were at an extreme end of the county, a slightly larger fee would be assessed. The office visit fees charged by his colleagues in Monticello in 1986 ranged from $20 to $75, and none of them make house calls. When he stopped delivering babies in 1981, Dr. Roberts' delivery fee was $150.

Currently Dr. Roberts has office hours the mornings of Monday, Tuesday, Thursday, and Saturday. The reduction in office hours has evolved gradually since his eightieth birthday, but only death will stop him completely from seeing patients.

On a typical day four or five patients will come to his house each afternoon for treatment, unannounced. He also deals with many patients by telephone during the afternoon and evening. One afternoon, when I was there, during a two hour period of time he worked with three patients by telephone. I was in his home for four hours one Friday, a day off, and he saw five patients who arrived at the house unannounced. He also conversed with eight patients by telephone during that same period of time.

Dr. Roberts´ fair treatment policy and excellent medical care which he began offering in Wayne County in the 1930´s have worked. He has treated thousands of individuals and families in his private practice since he began in 1939.

Places

Dr. Roberts´ travels to make house calls have taken him to every corner and crevice of Wayne County. He bought his first four-wheel drive Jeep in the 1940´s and has purchased a new model as each one wore out. There are places that he has driven which only a Jeep with four-wheel drive could possibly make the trip. But there also are places where he has made house calls that even his Jeep could not go. He would drive as far as he could and then a member of the family would meet him with a horse or mule, and he would ride it up the side of the mountain to the house. Other times he would leave his Jeep at the end of the road, if you could call what he was driving on a road, and walk one to three miles to a patient's house.

A typical situation would be for a patient to call and need Dr. Roberts to come to the house to see him. If this were a new patient or Dr. Roberts had not previously been to this patient's house he would ask where the patient lived.

"Well, Doc, I live in Slickford about three miles beyond Aus Brown's place. Do you know where that is?"

Dr. Roberts knew where Aus Brown's place was but "about three miles beyond" covered a lot of territory. Either he would request or the patient's family would volunteer someone to meet him at the road where he could leave his Jeep and they would guide him to the house.

Dr. Roberts has made house calls in the communities of Hidalgo, Stop, Susie, Powersburg, Number 1, Number 2, Cooper, Frazer, Coal Bank Mountain, Mount Pisgah, Rocky Branch, Oil Valley, Jennings Hollow, Shearer Valley, Harmon Hollow, Duncan Valley, and Griffin. These places received their names in a variety of ways. There may have been a country store or post office or both in a locality where several homes were within a few miles of each other. There may have been a school house in an area where children from a four or five mile radius attended school and the community was identified by the name of the school. Other places were identified by the families who settled there such as Duncan Valley, Harmon Hollow, Shearer Valley, Cooper, and Frazer.

Locating patients' homes in many of these communities is difficult in the bright noonday sun of summer. Finding them at two o'clock in the morning in the dead of winter would seem to be impossible, but Dr. Roberts has found them all hours of the day and night. When patients have needed him, he has gone where they were to care for their physical well-being.

The Visit and The Billing

Dr. Roberts has never made an appointment with a patient nor sent a patient a bill. When he began his practice, if people needed to see the doctor, they went to his office and waited their turn. If they were too sick to come to the office, they sent someone to town to ask the doctor to come to see them. Later, when the telephone came into popular use, they would call the doctor or have a neighbor call him and ask him to come to the house.

Making appointments was not the custom of physicians when Dr. Roberts began his practice, and he has never found it necessary to use an appointment system. This approach suited Dr. Roberts' relaxed style of working and relating to patients and has been satisfactory with his patients.

Patients go to Dr. Roberts' office and are seen on a first come first serve basis unless the situation is an emergency. The average length of time a patient has to wait is fifteen minutes unless there is a flu epidemic or in earlier years, if Dr. Roberts were called away to deliver a baby. When there was a flu epidemic a patient might have to wait for forty-five minutes or an hour but never more than an hour. Of course, if Dr. Roberts were called to deliver a baby, he might be gone several hours. When this was the situation usually patients would leave and return several hours later to see him.

Dr. Roberts' normal routine has been to see patients in the morning and the early afternoon in the office. Then, house calls are made in the afternoon. Usually when he returned home in the evening from making house calls there would be one or more patients waiting at his house to see him. Dr. Roberts referred to these as his "drive-in practice" and jokingly has said that he lived off his drive-in practice and put the money in the bank from his office practice. No doubt there were people who went to the house rather than to the office because they thought the waiting time would be less at the house than at the office.

On occasion there have been impatient patients. Considering only themselves, they expected to be seen immediately, but once they were in the doctor's office they were in no hurry to leave. Often those who apparently had the most time were the least willing to wait their turns and once their turns came were the most difficult with whom to terminate.

Some patients, thinking their condition merited it, thinking only about themselves, or not thinking, have just opened the door to his office and walked in. Some patients go in before their turns when another patient has left his office. Others have gone in when another patient was still in the office being examined by him.

Naturally there are patients who need attention more than anything. A little time and interest will work miracles for them. And there are patients who need to have the doctor find something wrong and treat the problem before they will ever feel better. One such situation occurred with a patient who was complaining about her ear hurting. Dr. Roberts washed out her ear several times, was unable to find any symptoms that would be causing pain in her ear, but the patient continued to complain. After several ear washings without much success of relief as far as the patient was concerned, he picked up a fish hook he had removed from another patient, dropped it in the basin, then invited the patient to look at what he had found. She immediately left the office relieved.

One patient who was notorious for needing to see Dr. Roberts for the most minor ailments also absorbed a large amount of time. On one such occasion when she continued to stay and stay in his office, the receptionist explained the situation to Mildred Tuttle who happened to be in her husband's office next door. Mildred said she needed to see Dr. Roberts. The receptionist knocked on Dr. Roberts' door and told him there was someone in Dr. Tuttle's office who needed to see him. The notorious patient left, and Dr. Roberts managed to see several other patients who needed him before the end of the day.

At different times during his career Alma has served as receptionist. As each of the girls got old enough, high school and college age, each one worked in the office during the summer as receptionist. JoAnn Anderson served as receptionist for Doctors Tuttle and Roberts for many years and Aleta Roberts has been Dr. Roberts' receptionist for the past eighteen years.

When he makes house calls or patients come to his house to see him, Dr. Roberts makes notes on a small piece of paper and then gives it to the receptionist to transfer to the office files. Sometimes he can't read his own writing. The receptionist often can read his writing better than he. He urged me in the first letter I received from him regarding this book, "If you decide to write this book about me, don't say anything about my penmanship."

Medicare and Medicaid require the doctor to do a large amount of paper work and record keeping. Dr. Roberts makes notations about patients and writes down their card number when he sees them in their homes or in his office. Twenty-five percent of the patients he sees would never see a doctor or receive any medical treatment were it not for Medicare and Medicaid. In spite of the excessive record keeping involved, Dr. Roberts continues to see these patients because he is convinced they need medical attention. He could hardly be seeing these patients for the money, since his fee is $10 or $15, depending on where he sees the patient. He would be justified to charge much more according to the current standards of the medical profession as well as the amount that he could be reimbursed from Medicare and Medicaid. For example, a registered nurse who makes a home visit receives $50 and a licensed practical nurse receives $30.

One unique business practice of Dr. Roberts is that he has never sent a bill to anyone. He is convinced that people who owe him for medical services know that they owe him. If they forget, they will remember the next time they need his services. He believes in the basic honesty of people. If they are going to pay they will when they have the money, and if they do not intend to pay him, then sending them monthly statements won't make them pay him. Actually, sending statements would cost Dr. Roberts time, energy, and postage.

One unusual situation did cause him to wonder. He had made a late night house call and after he finished seeing the patient was unable to wake the man of the house. Dr. Roberts was convinced the man was pretending to be asleep so he wouldn't have to pay the fee.

When I was interviewing Dr. Roberts at his home on a Friday morning, the doorbell rang. He went to the door and returned in a few minutes and announced, "There's still a few honest people in this world! That woman came by to pay me $10 she owed for an office visit from last week."

Here was a living illustration that confirmed what he has believed and practiced throughout his medical career.

People

Doctoring cannot happen in a vacuum. It involves the care of people. Dr. Roberts is full of stories, and people enjoy sharing stories about Dr. Roberts. The following accounts were mailed to me, told to me in person, or told by Dr. Roberts during the three days I made house calls with him.

Having delivered more than 4,400 babies means that many events of Dr. Roberts' practice revolve around the births of some of these babies and unusual circumstances related to them. His most prolific delivery work occurred during World War II when he delivered thirty-three babies in one month in addition to the care he gave to other patients. He has delivered three generations of children in two families in Wayne County, and he has delivered his share of twins; one year he delivered three sets in four days. But one thing he never accomplished was delivering a set of triplets. Certainly the most unusual twins' story is that of the five sets of twins born to Preston and Rosalie Bell. Dr. Roberts delivered four of the sets of twins and would have delivered the fifth, except a neighbor, in her hurry to get a doctor, called the wrong doctor. Dr. Roberts delivered two sets of twins to this couple in the same year, one set in February and another in December.

Dr. Roberts delivered a few babies in the hospital when he was in medical school working at Louisville City Hospital. He also delivered a few at St. Joseph's Hospital in Lexington during his internship. But prior to the opening of the

Wayne County Hospital in 1973, he delivered more than 4,000 babies in homes.

When he began his practice he would go to the home of a woman in labor when a family member contacted him. Sometimes he would be at the house many hours. Occasionally he would spend what was left of the night with the family because it was easier, and he would get more rest than trying to return home. In the morning the family would prepare breakfast for him. Country ham is his favorite.

One time he had two women who were in labor at the same time, but they lived about ten miles apart. He did not want either of them to know the other one was in labor because each would want him to stay with her. What did he do? He drove back and forth between their houses checking on each patient, not letting either know that another woman was in labor. Their babies were born about two hours apart. Ironically, three years later the same scenario with the same women was repeated.

Ride with Dr. Roberts through different sections of Wayne County and he will point to first one house and then another where he has delivered babies. He will tell you that he delivered a little girl over there and now she is a nurse or another one here is a laboratory technician. He pointed to one house saying he delivered a baby in that house late one night. "They didn't have any electricity so I drove my Jeep up to the edge of the porch and turned the lights on so I could see what I was doing." Then he added that the woman was wearing long underwear, and he asked her if she would like to change into a gown. She said, "No. There's a hole down there. It'll come out okay."

As Dr. Roberts and I went bouncing along the country road in his Jeep, he said, "I parked my

Jeep right here by the side of the road one time." This was as close as he could get to the house. He then walked about two miles up the side of the hill to get to the house where the family lived. The land is rough and the people rugged. When he arrived at the house, it was obvious the woman was in labor. Attempting to build some rapport with the woman, he asked her, "Well, do you want a boy or a girl this time?" Immediately the woman shot back at him, "I hope it's a damn wildcat and takes to the woods as soon as it's born!"

As we rode along he pointed to a house at the base of a hill and said that Dr. Rankin had been there all day on a labor case and the baby had not been born. He called for Dr. Roberts and said, "Get some chewing gum and cigars and come up here." He did. They were there several hours until the baby was born.

"I spent all day delivering a baby right there," he said, pointing to a house between the road and the creek as we wound our way around the mountain.

Signalling toward another house he told of a slow labor, and he became extremely tired. Just after he laid down on the floor to rest, the woman's husband told him, "You'd better be careful, Doc, the chinks (bed bugs) might get you."

"I got up and there were chinks all over the floor. I decided I wasn't as tired as I had thought."

During World War II, he delivered a baby to a lady whose husband had arranged a furlough from the Army to come home for the birth of his child. After the baby was born, he refused to go back to the Army and hid out in the hills for the remainder of the war. The authorities caught him after the war had ended.

As we crossed a creek he was reminded of one of his "wild goose chases."

> One time I went in the middle of the night on a call up to Denney's Hollow. It had been raining hard and the creek was up to the road. My car drowned out and one of the kinfolk of the woman who was having a baby was with me. I was close to a fellow's house, and he helped pull my car out with his mules. We drove on up to the woman's house where the baby was to be born, and the woman was not in labor, so all of that was in vain.

Of course the conditions have not always been the most sanitary or the most comfortable for mother, baby, or the doctor. In one home he delivered a baby where the room was so cold that steam rose off the baby when it was born. In another situation the mother's feet became frost bitten while she was giving birth to her child.

Abnormal situations did arise like the baby whose abdominal wall had not closed during the pregnancy. After delivering the baby, Dr. Roberts asked for a towel, wrapped the baby in it, and sent the baby to the Somerset Hospital thirty miles away. The baby survived and now has children of her own delivered by Dr. Roberts.

In 1942 Dr. Roberts arrived at the home of Corbin and Eva Lee Frost at 3:00 p.m. to deliver a baby. He did not leave until mid-morning of the next day. After being there awhile he hung his tie on a nail and made himself at home. The baby was stillborn. He told Eva Lee he had done everything he could to save the baby. Eva Lee concluded, "The thing that made you feel better was you knew that he really had." Over the years he delivered four healthy girls to Corbin and Eva Mae Frost. He also delivered their first grandchild.

One of the most difficult situations with which Dr. Roberts had to deal was the result of the placenta being born first. Because of this the mother bled to death and the baby died too. I asked him what he said to the family at a time like that. He replied, "I´m not very good at consoling people." I don´t know that any of us are good at consoling people, but one thing that Dr. Roberts has done well throughout his medical practice has been to stay with people, to be beside them when he was needed. He did not abandon them in their grief when death invaded their lives. There really is not anything better that anybody can do for another at such a time. Action like this endears a doctor to his patients and to their families.

The year was 1946 and Kathryn Ramsey was expecting a baby. Her two older boys caught the whooping cough. Six weeks before her third son was born, Kathryn got the whooping cough, and as a result was given little hope that the baby she was carrying would live. The chances were great that either it would be stillborn or have the whooping cough. But a lively, healthy boy was born at five o´clock. Dr. Roberts gently bathed and dressed the baby and laid him in his mother´s arms. Then he told Kathryn that he would have to go home, read some of his medical books to learn if he could give a newborn a shot. He returned to the Ramsey home at ten o´clock and told the family he could give the newborn four shots, one every other day. Kendall Koger Ramsey did not catch the whooping cough but grew from an infant into adulthood and now serves as the pastor of a Baptist congregation in Wayne County. Kathryn

Ramsey is convinced that Dr. Roberts used the skills and ability that God gave him to save her infant son's life.

Dr. Roberts delivered six of the eight children born to his brother-in-law and sister-in-law, Harley and Minnie Dolen. One of those children, Carolyn Needham, recalled the excitement and anticipation that filled their home when their dad would announce that he was going to get Uncle Mack that day, and they might have a new brother or sister when the children arrived home from school. Frances Dolen was the school teacher at the Huffaker School and boarded with the Harley Dolen family. When the time arrived for the birth of another child, not only was Frances the school teacher, but she also became the babysitter until everything was in order at home. Whenever a child was born to Harley and Minnie, the older children thought their Uncle Mack had brought the baby in his black bag. They wondered how the baby could breathe in that bag and why their mother was in bed after Uncle Mack "delivered" the baby.

Dr. Roberts delivered his first baby in the Wayne County Hospital on December 12, 1973, only fourteen years ago. At that time there was a cotton shortage which resulted in the hospital not receiving all the "surgical greens" that were needed. Here is JoAnne Crain's description of Dr. Roberts just prior to delivering his first baby in the new hospital:

> I was in the delivery room and looked up. There he stood with this dumb little green cap just sitting on top of his thinning hair. We didn't have any scrub shirts, so he just wore his undershirt. The next layer was a pair

of extra large scrub pants. To say the least, he was a peculiar sight. He had scrubbed and with hands in the air, I thought he was gonna loose those pants. He looked around the room and stated,
"Where did you get all this fancy stuff to have a baby with?"
I said, "Would you feel better if I got you some newspapers and a kitchen table and a large pan?"
"Yes, I think I would," he said. And very calmly he proceeded to gown up and deliver the baby.[4]

He delivered his last baby there on May 8, 1983. He delivered 341 babies at the Wayne County Hospital before he stopped practicing obstetrics. He enjoyed filling in for Dr. Frank Duncan when Dr. Duncan had to be out of town. He would enjoy telling Dr. Duncan when he returned, "I delivered two of your babies while you were gone."

Obstetrics is a straining practice, primarily because it involves all hours of the day or night and often many hours for each delivery. Dr. Roberts continued in obstetrics for an amazingly long time and might still be doing it if Alma had not insisted that he give up that part of his practice. Of course, she had to insist for five years before he quit. There is no longer a physician in Wayne County who delivers babies. A birthing service is available and midwives deliver the babies. This is upsetting to Dr. Roberts because the main reason for opening the hospital in Wayne County was to provide adequate health care for the births of babies.

In addition to delivering babies, Dr. Roberts also has been involved with many families in giving the babies names. It has not been uncommon for families to ask him for suggestions. When the Beverly Hillbillies was a popular television show, he suggested Jethro to several families who had boys. On other occasions he would suggest that a boy be named William Joseph, taking the names from Bill Tuttle and Joe Back who had offices on the same floor as his. Eula Bertram lived in the Cooper section of Wayne County, and she often assisted Mack with the delivery of babies. If the baby were a girl and the family asked Dr. Roberts what they should name her, he often would say, "Eula is a pretty name." In Cooper there are many women named Eula.

    Another family asked for his suggestion for their daughter's name and he recommended Nadine JoAnn. Nadine was the receptionist in the optometrist's office and JoAnn was Dr. Roberts' receptionist. The family responded that they liked Nadine but they didn't care for JoAnn.

    Of course many boys have been named Mack, and Dr. Roberts said, "Whenever a family named their new baby boy, Mack, I knew I wasn't going to get paid for delivering him."

    Knowing how the body functions and what medications to prescribe are important, but a doctor also needs to rely on common sense and intuitive insight. Early in his practice, Dr. Roberts was called to see a baby whose temperature was 106 degrees. The baby was having convulsions and it was the middle of winter. Dr. Roberts soaked a towel in ice water and wrapped it around the infant. (At that time this treatment would not have been possbile in the summer becasue ice was not readily available.)

    "That did the trick. In a short time the baby's temperature dropped down to 103 degrees and the convulsions stopped. I don't know if that was good medicine or not." He learned to trust his instincts.

Orthopedics also has been part of Dr. Roberts' medical practice. He has set simple fractures, but when patients had compound fractures he sent them to Somerset. At six years of age this writer broke his leg, and Dr. Roberts rode with the family to the hospital thirty miles away. More than thirty years later when he was asked why he didn't set the broken bone, without reviewing the chart, Dr. Roberts quickly replied, "Because the break was near the ankle, and if you don't get the bone set just right when the ankle is involved, you're likely to get a stiff joint." No stiffness ever developed.

Dr. Roberts began his medical practice before there were antibiotics. He had to treat people's symptoms. He would take care of the patients the best he could and let nature take its course. Treating people with pneumonia before the development of penicillin was an especially difficult medical problem. "Their fever usually broke on the fifth, seventh, or ninth day. Why it was on the odd days, nobody could tell."

During the pre-penicillin days a man brought his daughter, who had pneumonia and was running a high fever, to see him. He told this troubled father in his sensitive, caring tone, "I don't think she's going to make it, but her only chance is for you to get her to the hospital as quickly as you can." The girl did live, but blindness resulted from the high fever that had lasted for several days.

His medical practice also predated the existence of the modern communication device, the telephone. In those days when a sick person could not come to the doctor, a neighbor or family member would travel to town to tell Dr.

Roberts. He would finish seeing the patients who were waiting in the office and then drive out to the home of the patient who had sent for him. Twice during those years when he was gone for eighteen hours or longer, Alma went looking for him. She found him each time at the home of the person he had gone to see. The patient's need was such that it was a wiser use of his time to stay than to return to town and then go back the next day to see the patient. He had no way of getting a message to Alma to explain the situation to her.

Several years ago Robert Sexton was bitten by a copperhead, and Dr. Roberts went to his house to give him a shot. Dr. Roberts asked Robert if he killed the copperhead. "No. But I'm going back tomorrow and look for him." He did, found the snake, and killed it.

In the 1940's rapid transportation was not even in the dreaming stages, especially in some of the remote sections of the county. Emergency vehicles were a luxury found only in the big cities. When an accident occurred, family members would treat the injury until someone could get the patient to the doctor or could send for the doctor to come to the house.

On a warm, summer, Saturday afternoon, Harley and Minnie Dolen went to town, leaving the children to care for themselves at home for awhile. The kids were playing hide and seek and Jim took refuge in an apple tree in the orchard. In his hurry to hide, his foot slipped, and he promptly fell to the ground. His yelling and wailing could be heard for miles around and his brothers and sisters knew that he was seriously hurt. Jack and Carolyn had been left in charge in their parents' absence. They formed a packsaddle, carried Jim to the front porch, and waited for their parents to return. No one at their house took refuge in bed during the day. The bed was for sleeping and that was to be done only at night. By the time Harley and Minnie returned home the swelling in Jim's leg had become pronounced. Harley made a splint for Jim's broken leg and made a bed for him in the room where he and Minnie slept. Minnie sent some of the children to the creek to fill bags with sand and these were placed carefully around the injured leg. After the emergency had subsided Harley went for Dr. Roberts. After he arrived, he felt around on Jim's leg, examined the splint and sand bags closely, looked up at Minnie and Harley, and with the characteristic wry smile across his face announced, "I couldn't have done better myself!"

Refusing to treat patients has never been an option for Dr. Roberts. He didn't want to tell them a lie or have his wife lie to them about him suggesting he wasn't home or couldn't see them. In many ways this endeared him to his patients. It also contributed to intrusions because people knew that Dr. Roberts would not refuse to see them, no matter when they needed him.

Receptionists who have worked for Dr. Roberts have commented on his easy-going nature with employees and patients alike. Referring to his patients one receptionist said, "He's had some corkers over the years," but no one has ever heard him say an unkind thing to a patient or an employee. He is kind and can say anything to patients, and they never get upset. The reason is a combination of the manner in which he says things and his concern for his patients. Many people come to him to discuss marriage and family difficulties and other problems that have nothing to do with physical ailments; and yet, recent research does indicate that people's emotional conditions affect their physical well-being and vice versa.

One aspect of Dr. Roberts' practice for many years was doing blood tests, required by Kentucky law until recently, for couples who were applying for marriage licenses. In at least one situation Dr. Roberts told the young man that his fiancee's blood did not test well, indicating she had syphilis. The young man said, "I know, Doc. But I want to marry her anyway."

A second couple came in for their blood tests and wanted to charge the $5 fee for the test. Apparently they had not planned far ahead regarding the finances involved in being married. Dr. Roberts had some reservations about how well they would survive if they were going to begin their marriage by charging the fee for their blood tests.

Dr. Roberts was called to a home to see a three year old child that had a fever and nothing seemed to be working to help him get better. There were several women in the house. As often is the case, each person had her diagnosis of what was wrong with the child. One woman said, "I'll tell you what's wrong with that youngin'. He's having a nervous breakdown."

I went with Dr. Roberts to a call on a female patient in her late fifties. He checked her blood pressure and her heart rate and immediately told her that her blood pressure was okay at 140/80 and encouraged her to continue taking the pills he had prescribed. He told her I was writing a book about him. She said she had heard about it on the radio and commented, "I hope to live to see your book." She pointed out a huge picture on the wall of Paris and told me that Dr. Roberts told her during one of his visits that he had been to the place in the picture.

When the telephone first came into use there were party lines. When Dr. Roberts would arrive at the patient's home he would discover several neighbors had gathered there for him to see them because they overheard on the telephone that he was coming to their community. On other occasions neighbors would recognized his Jeep at a patient's home and drop in for him to treat them. While we were in the woman's home mentioned in the previous paragraph, her neighbor came into the house. He asked, "Doc, how much do you charge to take somebody's blood pressure?"

"Oh, about a nickel."

"All I've got is a quarter."

"I can probably make change."

The young man put his quarter back in his pocket and sat down in the chair next to Dr. Roberts. The young man was 21 and his blood pressure was 150/90 which is high for someone his age. Dr. Roberts asked him, "If I gave you a prescription for pills for your blood pressure, could you get it filled?"

Nothing more was said about payment as the young man took the prescription and said, "Yeah, I think my mom can get it filled."

One place where Dr. Roberts went to make a house call had a buck sheep that was known to charge and butt people. It was early morning, a heavy frost was on the grass, and Dr. Roberts was wearing rubber overshoes. He picked up a hickory tobacco stick to carry with him as he walked across the field. Here is his description of what transpired.

> Pretty soon I met the gentleman. He charged at me. I stepped aside and hit him on the nose with the tobacco stick. He kept charging and I kept hitting until I

>   bloodied his nose. All of a sudden
>   he walked away. I didn't follow
>   him to see where he was going.

Another version of this story had Dr. Roberts chewing tobacco. When the buck sheep charged him, the doctor stepped aside, grabbed the sheep by the wool on his head, and spit tobacco juice in both of its eyes. This is untrue because Dr. Roberts never chewed tobacco. Often stories are embellished or passed on incorrectly, hearing tobacco instead of tobacco stick. A well-known or revered person may easily become a legend.

During the years when Dr. Roberts' office was above Rankin's Drugstore, cough syrup came in gallon containers. Although there were several different names, there wasn't much difference in the cough syrup except the ones that contained codeine. Doctors would prescribe first one and then another type requiring the druggist to have several gallon containers of cough syrup opened at the same time. When Dr. Roberts would come through the drugstore, the druggist would tell him that he was overstocked on a certain type of cough syrup. For several days Dr. Roberts would prescribe that type cough syrup for patients with colds who needed a prescription.

In addition to being the physician for many of the citizens of Wayne County, Dr. Roberts also has been the primary doctor for members of his family. When his mother, father, and father-in-law were alive he provided medical care for them. In addition to visiting with them each Sunday afternoon, he also checked their blood pressure and heart rate to keep up with how they were physically.

Dr. Roberts also treated his own children. When they had medical needs that he could meet without them getting too upset, he would treat them. He dreaded giving them their regular vaccinations because they would crawl under the table to get away from him. He decided they should have Dr. Frank Duncan give them their vaccinations. When Marilyn needed a tonsillectomy, he was considering doing it, but a doctor in Somerset said, "Don't do that. Bring her up here, and I'll take out her tonsils." Most of the time from that point on he involved other doctors, at least in consultation, in treating his children. He also has treated his grandchildren and is preferred by them as Tara's story told in chapter five clearly indicates.

In addition to being the primary physician for his children, Dr. Roberts also included them in the practice as they got older. Ann remembers:

> I was, of course, always readily able to observe Daddy's relationship with his patients because we constantly had patients coming to the house, and he would let us kids "sit in" on the interesting cases. We particularly liked to watch him sew up cuts which he would do with a steady hand.[5]

At one point in their lives Alma decided that she would protect Mack from his patients. He was being interrupted at every meal. She thought if she screened the patients on the telephone or at the door to the house, this would help. A patient came to the door. Alma told the patient that Dr. Roberts was eating and could not see him then. The patient said, "You just tell him who it is. He has never turned me down."

Another time he had had little or no sleep for three consecutive nights. He was gone on a house call late at night when Alma received a call from a patient wanting the doctor to come to see him. Alma explained to the man that the doctor hadn't had any sleep and she doubted if he would make another house call after he got in from this one. Once again the confidence was expressed, "You just tell him who called. He'll come."

In 1960 Dr. Roberts began suffering from angina. There were times when the pain was severe. Alma once again was trying to shield him from some of the patient demands. A man came to the house and wanted to see the doctor. Alma explained to him that Dr. Roberts had angina and was not feeling well. The man responded, "I've got the same thing. Just don't pay any attention to it." From that time on Alma decided not to attempt to screen his patients. She would let the doctor handle his patients. That has suited him, and I know it has pleased his patients.

There also were times when Dr. Roberts' daughters felt the need to protect him. The most serious situation involved Marilyn. Not too many years ago, two men brought a third man to see Dr. Roberts late at night. They were rough looking men, unshaven and loud talking. The patient had a bad cut on the inside of his leg and the claim was that he had fallen out of a bunk bed when they were camping at the lake. Alma was worried and called the police. The police drove by the house several times but did not stop. Marilyn came out of her room toting a twenty-two rifle and three shells. Her mother asked, "What are you doing with three shells?"

"There are three of them, aren't there?"

Fortunately for everyone concerned in this frightening situation, the patient's needs were legitimate. The accident had happened as the men had said. But "Annie Marilyn Oakley" was prepared and confident.

Wayne County Hospital

Dr. Roberts was a member of the original medical staff of the Wayne County Hospital. He was delighted to have a hospital in Wayne County primarily for safer and more sanitary delivery of babies than for any other single reason. He felt that child delivery was a service that should be provided for people.

JoAnne Crain served as a registered nurse at the hospital. One of her first responsibilities was to hand deliver lists of equipment and supplies to the physicians in Wayne County so they could choose what was needed for the hospital. This was her first encounter with Dr. Mack Roberts. It was, as most first meetings are with him, quiet.

The big question for JoAnne and the others on the nursing staff at the hospital was, "Would Dr. Roberts participate at the hospital or was he too old?" At that time he was seventy. The Wayne County Hospital opened on December 3, 1973 at 8:00 a.m. Central Standard Time. At 8:20 a.m. the telephone rang at the hospital and on the other end of the line was Dr. Mack Roberts with a question, "How do I get somebody in down there?" The question of the nursing staff was answered when this vital participating country doctor admitted his first patient to the hospital. Later that morning he entered the hospital, found Joanne Crain, took her off to the side, and instructed her, "Whatever my patients need, you girls give it to them."

Often patients become extremely uneasy about their condition and have an anxiety reaction which is disturbing to all concerned. Patients admitted in the emergency room often are in various states of hyperventilation, hand wringing, crying, and near total breakdown. Dr. Roberts' easy going nature often has a calming effect in situations like this. JoAnne Crain oberserved this with patients in the emergency room.

> These patients require a nurse who is well trained and experienced in psychiatric therapy, and above all, a good listener. Many times however, at the hospital after much exasperation on the nurse´spart, the arrival of Dr. Roberts was the cure. Why was he so effective? What did he do? He would just walk in and stand there. All the valium in the hospital could not calm a patient like the presence of Dr. Roberts. [6]

Alma also gives testimony to Mack's calm approach when patients are in trouble. She said that if he were stopped by a state policeman it will take him an hour to find his driver's license because he gets so nervous. But if somebody loses a battle with a chain saw and blood is gushing everywhere on everybody, he is just as cool as can be.

The worst medical catastrophe to which Dr. Roberts has been called was to the home of a man and his two sisters. The three of them had attempted suicide by slitting their throats. When Dr. Roberts arrived the room was splattered with blood. With his help two of the three survived, but it was a gruesome, messy, horrifying experience.

Doctor/Patient Relationship

There is more to medicine than diagnosis and prescriptions. A personal touch and caring for the individual are important for the healing and health of people. Most of the time Dr. Roberts has had to treat the family as well as the patient. Contemporary medical practice focuses more on the concept of wholistic medicine which he has been practicing all along but without identifying it as such. His conversations with other members of the family when making a house call or when a patient was in his office gave attention to other family members and helped them feel value and worth. His interest in how one family member was doing in caring for another helped that person to know he or she was not alone in this ordeal.

Dr. Roberts has continued to learn about medical procedures and the care of patients throughout his practice. He has learned the most about being a physician from his experience of treating people, reading medical journals, and attending medical meetings. He has done an excellent job of continuing his education throughout his career, a compliment to him and a benefit for his patients.

The attention that he has given some of his patients has been as important, on many occasions more important, than any diagnosis or treatment he would prescribe. He enjoys making house calls because he is helping people. The people are appreciative. For many people it is the highlight of their week, maybe even of the month, for the doctor to come to their houses. Seldom is an apology made or an expression of concern given about the appearance of the house. They are just delighted that he cared enough to stop to see them.

Patients do not know exactly when Dr. Roberts is going to come to their homes. They call him about their condition, and if it is not an emergency situation, he tells them he will stop by in a day or two when he is out that way. He doesn't make any notes about whom he needs to see or about whom he had told he would go see. "I just remember that I'm going to see them. I try to forget it, but I can't."

Dr. Roberts has a delightful sense of humor that has served him well for more than eight decades. I asked him, "Where did you get your sense of humor?"

"I didn't know I had one," was his immediate reply.

He teases with his patients. A man will come in without any teeth and Dr. Roberts will say to him, "You ought to have your teeth pulled." Or before he gives a shot he will swab the patient's sleeve with a cotton ball as if he were going to give the shot through the sleeve. He gave medication to one woman and she asked, "What can I eat on this?" His immediate answer was, "Everything except bear and wild turkey."

His ability to see humor in life has helped him cope with some people and situations that have been trying, irritating, and frustrating as he has cared for patients. He summarized one situation this way, "Will Rogers said he never met a man he didn't like, but he never met Amp Gregory."

He has cared for several elderly men and women whose family members lived in other areas of the country. Some family members have questioned the type of medical care a relative was receiving and been eager to offer suggestions and comments about what treatment the patient receives. Dr. Roberts' summarized those experiences with this observation, "Those the furtherest away have the most advice."

Dr. Roberts has several older patients who come to see him periodically. Of course age is relative. At eighty-three he doesn't see himself as old, but some of his old patients are eighty-nine or ninety. When a woman who is that age comes in with an ailment he often will say to her, "The only thing wrong with you is you stayed out too late last night."

One of the times that Dr. Roberts took Dr. Rankin with him for consultation resulted in Dr. Rankin telling others about Dr. Roberts' prescription for the patient. Dr. Roberts was attempting to diagnosis the woman's disease so he would know what treatment to prescribe. He asked her several questions, and each question drew from the woman a long and involved discourse, most of which was unrelated to her presenting illness. As he finished the examination of the woman and was ready to leave he prescribed this remedy, "I'll tell you the best thing you can do is to keep your bowels open and your mouth shut."

As I traveled over the county with Dr. Roberts, we rode up to a small house that looked like it had been built on the only available flat piece of land. As he turned off the engine he said, "This woman has two retarded children. She has a rough time." We went to the door and the woman graciously invited us in. The room was small and dark with a low ceiling. The black and white television was on and the woman said she was trying to get some work done. The girls were asleep. Dr. Roberts walked back toward the tiny bedroom that had space for two single beds, one was a hospital bed, and a walk space between them. One girl was sitting up. Her mother said she must have heard us come in and woke up. The girls looked like they were ten and thirteen. I was shocked to learn they were twenty-nine and thirty. She has another daughter who is twenty-seven and works in town. This woman's husband left her many years ago, and it is a full time job to care for these two daughters at home. One is able to walk around in the house, but the other one is bedridden. In many ways this mother is a prisoner in her own house. It was obvious that Dr. Roberts has much compassion for this woman and her situation in life.

We traveled further and stopped at a neat little house on the side of the hill, got out of the Jeep, and walked into the yard. A man in his forties was painting the porch. Two other men were sitting on the edge of the porch. Dr. Roberts spoke to one man and asked him about the man sitting next to him, "Who's this boy?" (nodding toward a man who must have been in his seventies).

"Is Pearlie in the house?" Dr. Roberts asked.

"Yeah."

"Well, I better go raise Cain with Pearlie."

We walked around to the front of the house and stepped up on the porch. As Dr. Roberts approached the open door he said, "Pearlie, you in there?" She was, and invited us into the small, neatly kept kitchen. The kitchen had a few white enamel cabinets, a small refrigerator, a dinette set with four chairs, and a spotless wood cook stove. Pearlie was sitting in a chair by the dinette table and a walker was off to her left side. Dr. Roberts took off his light tan suede hat and laid it upside down on the table. He set his medical bag on the table, took out his stethoscope and his equipment for measuring blood pressure and checked Pearlie's blood pressure. Immediately he told her that her blood pressure was high, 190/80. He asked her if she were taking her medication for high blood pressure and she said she was taking one pill a day. "Better double it. I'll check on you in about a week." The woman indicated she might be in town in a few days.

"Okay. Come in the office or I'll come back to see you. We don't want you to mess around and have a stroke. You're watching how much salt you're eating and how much moonshine whiskey you're drinking, aren't you?"

"Yeah," the woman laughed. "You know I don't drink no moonshine, Doc." "How old are you, Doc?"

"I was thirty-two in the spring." (There may be times when he does feel about fifty years younger than he is.)

Making house calls does seem to invigorate him. Before we left he told Pearlie that he was eighty-two and would be eighty-three in July.

At one house where he made a call, the woman had two hen turkeys. Her gobbler had been killed on the road several weeks earlier. Before he left Dr. Roberts asked, "Have you gotten a gobbler yet?"

"No, I haven't been able to locate one."

"I've been trying to locate a gobbler for us," he interjected. "We need a gobbler. We need him right away. It's going to soon be turkey setting time."

In this conversation, Dr. Roberts not only identified with the woman's need for a gobbler, but her need became his and suddenly they were in turkey partnership. This interest in patients contributes greatly to the coping and healing processes for them.

He likes people, and this has contributed significantly to his enjoyment of his vocation, his relationships with his patients, and how he communicates with them. His enjoyment of people, his concern for them, and the Hippocratic Oath are three things that have contributed to his treating everyone who came to him until he was sixty-five or seventy years old. At that time, although he was not about to retire, he began to see the value in conserving his energy by reducing his work load.

Only in recent years have there been a couple of people that he refused to treat. One to whom he refused treatment was a man who was in his office with a bad knee. Dr. Roberts was attempting to treat his ailment by draining water from his knee. Suddenly the man went into a rage, began throwing things and knocking things off the desk. Someone in the adjoining office heard the uproar and called the police. About the time the police arrived the man settled down as suddenly as he had gotten upset. He apologized. The policeman said that it would be up to Dr. Roberts to decide what would be done. The man asked Dr. Roberts what he owed him and he responded, "If you get out of here and never come back, that is all you owe me."

The other patient that Dr. Roberts refused to treat never was confronted face to face with his refusal. One night he had been out late on a house call, had returned home about 2:00 a.m. and had just gotten to sleep when there was a loud banging on the door. It took Dr. Roberts a few minutes to get to the door. Just as he reached for the doorknob, he heard a man's voice on the other side saying, "Lay in there and sleep, you S.O.B." Instead of turning the doorknob, he withdrew his hand from the knob and went back to bed.

I asked Dr. Roberts, "Did you ever work with alcoholics?" "Yeah. Don't like 'em. One man went to Frank Duncan for treatment. Frank asked him why he didn't come to see me and the man said, 'He don't like drunks.'" Dr. Roberts said, "I never did like a drunk, especially a drunk woman." Although he did not refuse to treat patients because they were intoxicated, he did not have much sympathy for them and the condition that their abuse of alcohol may have caused.

There was a man who had been drinking alcohol and was in an automobile accident. His bald head had slammed into the windshield. He came to Dr. Roberts for treatment. Dr. Roberts had to pick many glass splinters out of the patient's scalp and then sew up some of the places, a stitch here and two or three there. Several times while being treated, the patient said, "Doc, I need another drink." Dr. Roberts responded, "Okay," and poured rubbing alcohol on the patient's head.

A patient came to Dr. Roberts' office who had spilled hot water on his lap, severly burning his penis. The patient had whittled a hole in a potato and inserted his penis in the hole to keep it cool. He asked Dr. Roberts what he should do, and Dr. Roberts replied, "Continue the therapy."

Dr. Roberts had a gentleman patient who frequently suffered from wierd seizures. Usually a placebo was as good as any dose of Valium. Often the man's neighbors would call Dr. Roberts to come see the man when he was having a seizure. On one visit he arrived and could see the patient "jerking away" on the kitchen table. Dr. Roberts went to both doors; they were locked. He tried the windows; locked. He could not get into the house. Finally he yelled at the fellow, "If you want me to take care of you, you're gonna have to open the door." The patient stopped his shaking and jerking, got off the table, walked over to the door, opened it so the doctor could get in the house, walked back to the table, laid down, and resumed his "seizure."

His care and treatment of patients has embraced about every possibility imaginable, including serving as dentist on at least one occasion. Sharing office space with a dentist and their patients using the same waiting room made this situation possible. A man who was intoxicated came to see Dr. Tuttle, and there were several patients to see the dentist. The man became irritated because of having to wait. Dr. Roberts told him, "I´ll pull that tooth for you." The man said, "Okay." Dr. Roberts got a pair of forceps and pulled the tooth. The man left relieved but returned a few minutes later and said that the wrong tooth had been pulled. He sat down and Dr. Roberts pulled another one. This time he got the right one. This dental patient was not given Novocain because it would have made him nauseous when it combined with the alcohol in his system. Dr. Roberts did what the dentist would have done except the dentist might have detected the right tooth to pull the first time.

Having made a late night house call, Dr. Roberts spent the remainder of the night with a family. The next morning he had breakfast with the family and was leaving the house when the man asked, "Doc, do you have anything for the itch? Every one of us here has got the itch." Doc itched all the way back to town, but he didn´t catch the disease.

Early one morning at Rupert Abbott´s store a woman fell going up the steps to the store and badly scraped her knee. Some of the people helped her into the store and gave her a place to sit down. They encouraged her to rest there and told her that Dr. Roberts would be by there soon and he could examine her knee. Not much time passed before he did come by, and someone stopped him and asked him to examine the woman. He did, her situation was not too serious, and as he finished the examination he took some Ginson Violet and painted a cat's head on her knee.

Such artistry has been a common practice of his with children. Often after examining a child he would asked the child to show him his belly button; using the umbilicus as the center of his art work and Ginson Violet as his paint he would draw a design that would stay with the patient for days, if not weeks. To say that Dr. Roberts is an artist is to use the term loosely, but no patient whose skin served as a canvas will ever forget the drawing done by the doctor's hand which communicated his interest by spending time tangentially related to the patient's medical needs.

In January of 1941 a man went to Dr. Roberts' hotel room in Monticello to get him to come to deliver a baby. It was two o'clock in the morning and the temperature was twenty degrees below zero. He went with the man and stayed all day until the baby was born between three and four o'clock that afternoon. Right after that Dr. Roberts caught the flu and was sick for several days. He still enjoys accusing this family of causing him to catch the flu in 1941. (Alma caught the flu from Mack and barely recuperated from it before their wedding.)

When interviewing Dr. Roberts I had the privilege of overhearing at least his side of conversations with patients who would call while I was there. One woman called and said she thought the medicine he had prescribed was making her sleepy. She wondered if that could happen. He said that it might be and asked how much she was taking. She was taking two tablets each time. He said, "Why don't you cut that in half? Just take one and see how that does." The patient was satisfied and agreed to try this approach for awhile.

Another woman called and was concerned about her blood pressure. She thought it was high. He said, "Your blood pressure was okay last week when you were in to see me."

"Yeah. Well, I think it's up now," I overheard her say.

"Next time I'm out that way I'll stop in and check it for you again."

"Okay. Do you think it's okay for me to go to church?"

"Yeah. Going to church won't hurt you. If you're goin' to conk out, that's a good place to go."

When Bill Tuttle was sick, had come home from the hospital, and then seemed to worsen, he didn't want to return to the hospital. Dr. Roberts didn't want to have to send him to hospital if it wasn't necessary. They were able to provide oxygen for Bill at home and Dr. Roberts went to see him every day. If he hadn't, Bill would not have been able to stay at home. In many ways it would have been easier on Dr. Roberts, physically at least, to have hospitalized Bill. This is one of many illustrations of his interest in and relationship to his patients which has benefited the patient. In this situation Bill Tuttle was able to remain at home and to die at home as he desired. Mildred's summarizing comment was, "If it had not been for Dr. Roberts, I would never have been able to keep Bill at home."

Many experiences have occurred during Dr. Roberts' practice that do not fall into the realm of medical practice as we think of it, such as the couple who wanted him to perform their wedding ceremony. He invited people from the dentist's office next door to come into his office. He said, "We need some witnesses. We're going to have a wedding." Then he took out a book that had yellowed sheets in it and he began, "Do you take this fair young maiden to be your lawfully wedded wife?" The man responded, "I do, Doc, I do." He continued through the marriage ceremony and then told the couple to go over to the courthouse and get married legally.

Keeping up with patients through the years has been a difficult if not impossible task unless they have continued as his patients. Naturally, many of his patients have moved away. Others have chosen another doctor for their family physician, and some haven't been to a doctor for years.

In the spring of 1986 Mack and Alma were driving across Mount Pisgah near the state line between Kentucky and Tennessee. At the top of the hill was a truck by the side of the road. As they came closer they saw a woman and couple of children in the truck. They stopped and began a conversation. In the midst of the conversation he asked the woman who she was and if she knew him. "Why sure, I know you Doc. You delivered me."

Several years earlier on a transatlantic trip that he and Alma took, they were sitting on the airplane at the airport in London. Someone tapped him on the shoulder and asked him if he were Mack Roberts. He said he was and the man told who he was, that he was in the Air Force and that Dr. Roberts had delivered him nearly forty years earlier in Wayne County.

Success

Dr. Roberts has been successful as a physician in every sense of the word. He has provided quality health care for people in Wayne County for more than fifty years. He has given of himself day and night for the benefit of his patients. He is respected by people throughout the county and by his colleagues in the medical field. He has provided well for his family both emotionally and financially. Money has not been paramount to him; yet, he has always had plenty of it to do with as he desired. One of his teachers in medical school, Dr. Ervin, told them in class, "Boys, if you're getting into this profession to get rich, you're in the wrong profession." The professor was not saying that they couldn't make much money as doctors. He was saying that their motivation for being doctors was wrong if it was to make money. Their motivation for being in the medical field should be to care for the health needs of people who came to them.

A tribute to Dr. Roberts is that financial remuneration has not been his goal as a physician. In the words of one professional man in Monticello, "Dr. Roberts has not sought financial reward and yet money has come to him."

Enormous medical bills are a recent development. At the time that Dr. Roberts was completing medical school, doctors often had patients who would not pay or were unable to pay or who resisted paying their doctors. One story being told at that time stated that a person would pay a lawyer $5,000 to keep him out of the gates of the penitentary but wouldn't pay a doctor $500 to keep him out of the gates of hell.

His honesty and truthfulness have contibuted as much to Dr. Roberts' success as a physician as has his ability to diagnose and treat patients' physical symptoms and diseases. He has not been one to pretend that he knew something when he didn't, and he has never attempted to bluff his way through with his patients. People know and appreciate these qualities in him, and this attitude endears him to them all the more.

He has been willing to seek consultation with a fellow physician or refer a patient to another doctor who has more expertise in an area than he. It is reported that Dr. Waggle of Somerset has said of Dr. Roberts, "If you can ever get a diagnosis out of Mack Roberts, you had better pay attention to it. Ninety-nine percent of the time he will be right."

One man was having difficulty breathing and went to see Dr. Roberts. In addition to the breathing problem, he told the patient his heart was beating too fast. He sent him to the hospital in Monticello for X-rays. Then he wanted to send him to Somerset for Dr. Waggle to care for him. The man said, "Now, I would just as soon you take care of me. You've taken care of me for all these years." Dr. Roberts said, "No. It's too complicated for me. You need to be in the hospital where Dr. Waggle can see you and take care of you." The patient spent several days in the hospital, his body eliminated the fluid, he was cured of what was causing the fluid build-up, and returned home. This is one example of the many times when Dr. Roberts recognized and admitted his limitations and through referral got proper care for one of his patients.

Hundreds of people in Wayne County will give witness to the generosity that Dr. Roberts has shown to them. Obie Corder's daughter was home from college one weekend and became ill on Sunday morning. Obie drove to the Elk Spring Valley Baptist Church, about five miles from his home. He asked an usher to ask Dr. Roberts to come out, which he did. Obie told him about Twyla, and Dr. Roberts followed Obie home to examine her. When Dr. Roberts completed his examination of Twyla, Obie gave him ten dollars. They talked a few minutes together. Then Dr. Roberts went over to say good-bye to Twyla and gave her the ten dollars to take back to college with her.

Many years earlier a family's son had double pneumonia. To treat the boy Dr. Roberts stopped in to see him every morning on his way to the office and every evening on his way home. During that time when he wasn't certain about the condition and situation of the boy, he brought Dr. Rankin with him to consult with him about the boy and his treatment. He made a total of nineteen visits to this home and never charged the family for them.

More than one person has asked Dr. Roberts what he owed him for the medical care, and knowing the person did not have to money to pay, Dr. Roberts has replied, "Vote Republican and go to the Baptist church." He has been known to add to some patients, "and do your banking at the Monticello Bank."

Dr. Roberts has been a physician to the poor people of Wayne County. He has provided medical care for people whether or not they could pay him or whether there was any prospect of paying him. He has said that his greatest pleasure in life has been "providing medical care for people who had no way to pay for it."

Dr. Roberts has easily and consistently communicated interest in his patients and what was best for them. His open, frank, honest manner with his patients has been appreciated throughout his practice. He communicates his concern to the people by the way that he relates to them, but he does not let his concern for them weigh him down emotionally, or bear heavily on his mind in a way that affects negatively his treatment of other people his relationship with his family, or the way he relates to friends, colleagues, and employees. Patients like Dr.

Roberts because of his good disposition. He is a friend to them and is willing to help in any way that he can.

Dr. Mack Roberts is comfortable and confident in his work as a physician. His calmness and self-control help put his patients at ease. He understands the pride of the people who make their homes in the hills and valleys of Wayne County. His service to those people far exceeds the medical attention he has provided, and his understanding and care for them may have contributed more to their healing and health than the medical expertise he has used in treating their diseases and injuries.

Dr. Roberts has been a most accessible doctor. His colleague, Frank Duncan, said that whenever Mack was in the county, he was available to the people who needed his attention. Immediate and extended family members give testimony to this in their comments that he never sat down to a meal without being interrupted. He never attended a family gathering without arriving late or leaving early because of the needs of one or more people. The time of day or the day of the week made no difference to him. Often his driveway was lined with several cars of patients who had come to see him after office hours. He has continued to live by the oath he took more than fifty years ago when he said he would prescribe "regimen for the good of my patients according to my ability and my judgment and never do harm to anyone." Every one of his patients believes that he has adhered to and lived that oath to the ultimate possibilities that any doctor could do.

Several characteristics of Dr. Roberts´ approach to the medical care of people surface. 1) Children are his favorites, and he probably is partial to girls. He always takes out time to blow up a balloon for children before "doctoring" them. And, if he meets any of his child patients on the street, he will say, "Let me see your tongue," and put a small piece of gum on it. He couldn't distribute gum or suckers in his office because Tuttle was such a fanatic about sugar causing tooth decay. Dr. Roberts was always on the sick child's side. One situation with Mrs. Marsh (school truant officer) illustrates this. She brought a little boy to him who said he was sick, but it was obvious that she doubted the boy's story. He was holding his side, and after examining him Dr. Roberts said, "This boy is hurting, I know, and should not be in school." The little boy had such a relieved look on his face, opposite from Mrs. Marsh's. 2) The drinking of alcohol and cursing were definitely not tolerated by him, and a woman smoking in his office was immediately told to take her cigarette out and then come back in to see him. 3) Dr. Roberts was genuinely interested in his patients and they knew that. They were convinced that he would not turn them down or refuse to check on them day or night regardless of where he had been or how tired he was. The typical response of a patient "Oh, just tell him who it is, and I know he will come," communicates the conviction that people had of his interest in them.

  Dr. Mack Roberts has been a general practicioner of medical care for more than fifty years in Wayne County. He was a joy to work with at the hospital, according to members of the hosptial staff. He was totally supportive of the administration and cooperative with the staff. He was well respected and appreciated by the staff and the patients because he gave much attention to the patients. He always had time to stop and talk with patients and with staff. He is a physician out of the old school of medical practice who continues actively to practice medicine for the people and for his enjoyment. He has gvien away an amazing amount of medical care, the amount no one knows, including Dr. Roberts.

He carries no malpractice insurance because the way he treats and relates to people he doesn't need it. The comment made by one nurse has been echoed by patients, colleagues, and family in a variety of complimentary ways, "God only made one Dr. Roberts."

In 1983 when Dr. Roberts celebrated his eightieth birthday, many citizens of Wayne County began expressing concern about loosing their doctor and who would take his place when Dr. Roberts either retires or dies. He is the only physician in the county who makes house calls, although no longer at night. There are people that would never see a doctor if he did not go to their homes to see them, and there is a sense in which Dr. Roberts' medical practice represents the end of an era in medicine. One patient summarized the feelings of many that Dr. Roberts treats, "If he were to quit, I don't think he would know what to do. I don't like to think about him not being around. I just put that out of my mind."

Although some have verbalized concern about Dr. Roberts' retiring, they really do not need to worry about that. As long as he is physically able and professionally astute, he will continue to practice medicine. This was illustrated in 1979 when he and Alma built a new house and included an office in it for him to see patients who came to the house. When they were quizzed about this, they responded in unison, "Sure we had an office put in this house." He never had one in the house on North Main Street. What this said was that at age seventy-six, Dr. Roberts was planning to continue his medical practice. At the time of this writing he was eighty-three and

I asked him, "When are you going to retire?"
"You mean voluntarily?"
"Yes."
"Got no plans."

Dr. Roberts has reduced his work load as a physician. In 1983 he quit delivering babies, and on July 1, 1985 he stopped admitting patients to the hospital and began taking off from work an additional day each week. Now when he has a patient who needs to be hospitalized, he refers the person to another doctor, usually J. K. Phillips, Jr.

The practice of medicine has continued to sustain Dr. Roberts because he loves medicine. There is an internal motivation that keeps him on the job. He has great care for the individual and his great love for people is why he has continued his medical practice. He will continue to practice medicine as long as he is giving quality care to patients. He knows himself and his abilities well and will know when the quality of his care begins to decline. I believe him when he describes his medical career with the one liner, "I've loved every minute of it."

Notes

[1] Betty Tuttle, Personal Letter, March 25, 1986.
[2] Helen Dees, Personal Letter, April 25, 1986.
[3] Ibid.
[4] JoAnne Crain, Personal Letter, March 30, 1986.
[5] Ann Looney, Personal Letter, April 8, 1986.
[6] Op. Cit.

Millard Jones and Mack Roberts in Rankin's Drug Store.

The Preston Bell family, who had five sets of twins.

Dr. Roberts and his receptionist, JoAnn Anderson

Dr. Roberts and his receptionist, Aleta Roberts.

7

I'D HATE TO BE THE RICHEST MAN
IN THE GRAVEYARD

Dr. Gamblin, a physician in Monticello when Dr. Roberts began his practice, was asked by a family if he would be willing to consult with Dr. Clark about the diagnosis and treatment of a woman, and he agreed he would. He arrived at the home where the woman lived and examined her. He was there about an hour before the other doctor arrived. The community had gathered and then people began to say, "There comes the doctor. There comes the doctor." The doctor had a long beard, knickers, and knee socks and was known as an herb doctor. Dr. Clark asked Dr. Gamblin what he thought was wrong with the woman. Dr. Gamblin said he thought she had tuberculosis of the bowels. Dr. Clark agreed and asked Dr. Gamblin if he had ever used a black cat poultice to treat such a case. Dr. Gamblin had to admit that he hadn't, and he realized right then that he fell out of favor with the crowd. Dr. Clark used a black cat skin poultice to treat the woman, and not long after this, the woman died. Several weeks later Dr. Gamblin saw Dr. Clark who was bemoaning the fact that the woman had died and said, "If I could have gotten there sooner and had a little blacker cat, I think I could have pulled her through."

It was in a climate of medical opinion like this that Dr. Roberts began his medical practice. Through the years he has gotten a bang out of things his patients have said to him, and he has been able to respond in kind to comments made to him, which has only deepened his relationship with his patients and endeared him to them. Yet, his reactions and responses to his patients have never degraded them. The following is a series of vignettes that give a flavor of what Doc has heard from his patients and how he has responded.

Patients' Comments

Patients have given self-diagnoses, suggested treatments and made observations about their conditions, using a vocabulary often known only to them. Dr. Roberts has been able to interpret their words and descriptions with understanding. He has accepted them and responded to their diagnoses, descriptions, and opinions without embarrassing or belittling them. Patients have identified their ailments as nartharitis or high blood. Some refer to having their blood pressure checked as taking their blood temperature. A 12 shot or a building shot is their vocabulary for a B 12 shot. One patient said she needed a penamycin shot, a coined word combining penicillin and Terramycin.

Self-Diagnosis

All of us diagnose our illnesses to some extent, giving names to various ailments. Dr. Roberts has heard them all. One patient identified his symptoms as having sore rafters, a reference to his ribs. Another patient was ill and said she really hadn't been well since she had the calopis. Dr. Roberts never did determine what calopis was. One woman said her husband was suffering from pisin kidneys. He asked her, "How do you know?"

"Dr. Sims," a reference to Dr. John Simmons, "said he did."

A woman who was having abdominal pain diagnosed her condition. "I got problems with my intentionals."

One man told Dr. Roberts he had "a bad kidney problem" and wanted some medicine for it. Dr. Roberts asked him what was wrong and the man said, "When my water hits the ground, it splatters." Doc replied, "Yeah, that's pretty bad!"

Important to patients in their diagnoses is to identify the cause of their illness. In this regard a man suffering prostatitis concluded he didn't know what had made him sick unless it was too many fogs in August.

One pregnant woman, on her way to the Wayne County Hospital, gave birth to her baby in the taxi. When Dr. Roberts saw her he asked why she waited until so late to go to the hospital and she said, "I didn't know when it was going to strike."

Home Remedies

Patients often attempt home remedies to cure themselves of their ailments. An old proverb suggests, "He who has himself for a patient has a fool for a doctor." Who hasn't experienced the truth of this proverb? After being unsuccessful with a home remedy, a patient may turn to the doctor for assistance. This was the situation with the parents of a child who had the chicken pox. They called Dr. Roberts to come to their home in the extreme edge of the county to see their child. After he arrived and began examining the child, he asked if they had tried any treatment. They had found a black chicken with "yaller legs," stretched the child across the doorway and made the chicken fly over him. Since that had not seemed to do the child any good, they called the doctor.

Another dimension to home remedies is the advice that people often are eager to give to others, but would never follow themselves. Here are two illustrations.

One man had an invalid wife for whom he was the main care giver. He tried to encourage her at times when she seemed depressed. Often his instructions to her would be, "Have faith and trust up." Once he became ill and was having severe abdominal pains. His wife encouraged him, "Have faith and trust up." To which he responded, "But this is too low in my stomach."

In another situation a woman suffered with high blood pressure. Her husband didn't feel that she needed any medication because he had his own treatment for her. He gave her some Sassafact (his term for sassafrass) tea. The man also had difficulty with high blood pressure. Dr. Roberts asked him, "Do you take Sassafact tea?"

"Oh I never touch the stuff myself," was his immediate response.

Patient Needs

Patients go to Dr. Roberts for things other than medical or health needs. Often they need the guidance of an older person, or they want the opinion of one who has dealt with many situations and conditions.

Because of these needs patients talk to Dr. Roberts about anything. He became a father substitute for one patient who said, "Ever since my dad died, I've gone to Doc Roberts when I needed advice."

Often a patient's conversation is unrelated to anything about his health. One of his male patients told him he had a hen that went to setting. Dr. Roberts asked, "Did you put any eggs under her?"

"No, I put potatoes under her." No one could determine the rationale for this action, but Dr. Roberts was a good ear, spending time with the patient talking about what the patient wanted to discuss.

Common in his practice are patients who want to talk with him about struggles and problems in their lives or to seek his advice on a variety of issues that may or may not relate to their physical health.

One woman talked to Dr. Roberts about her marriage. She had learned that her husband had been having an affair with another woman. She told Dr. Roberts, "I want to ask you a question. I'll do whatever you say, Doc. Should I sue him for divorce or kill him?" He suggested the less violent solution.

Observations

Patients are surprisingly free with their comments about their situations. Their observations may be blunt but often helpful and insightful for their conditions and needs. The following running commentary of exerpts from Dr. Roberts' encounters with some of his patients provides a glimpse at some of the observations they have made about themselves, family members, or friends.

A woman gave birth to a child and when the placenta passed she asked, "Did I lay an egg?"

One person explained the emotional stability of her family by saying, "We never did have any trouble with our nerves. We didn't cultivate them."

A woman patient that Dr. Roberts went to see was complaining about her situation. She said, "I didn't rest at all. I just terrified all night." And another said she was suffering from manifold when she meant menopause.

A few years ago Dr. Roberts was planning a trip to Europe and one of his patient's asked him, "Doc, are you going to fly or drive through?"

Elmer Pittman was a well known character in Monticello for many years who often preached on the courthouse lawn. He was a frequent patient of Dr. Roberts. Especially during the space flights to the moon Elmer was insistent that no one had ever been to the moon. Often a subject of discussion between Dr. Roberts and Elmer would be Dr. Roberts' insistence that he was going to the moon. He would tell Elmer that men had been to the moon, and Elmer would insist, "Oh Doc, nobody's ever been to the moon."

When Dr. Roberts was on a trip abroad, he sent Elmer a postcard written as if he were on the moon. Although Elmer didn't believe anyone had been to the moon, he quoted that card word for word all over town to everyone he met implying that Dr. Roberts had been to the moon. As far as Elmer was concerned, Doc hung the moon. Patients, like Elmer, really cared about Doc from the heart because Dr. Roberts cares about his patients from the heart and never makes any distinction between them because of where they live, who they are, what they say, or how they think. This attitude and approach in relating to patients has caused many of them to describe Dr. Roberts as a Christian gentleman.

When one of Dr. Roberts' older male patients was in his office, he asked him if he had any inclinations toward matrimony and the man responded, "Yeah. Right back here (pointing to his shoulder blade)."

Naturally there have been patients who were suspicious of things they did not understand or conveniences with which they were unfamiliar. He was giving a woman some medication in his office, and he went to the sink to get her some water. She said, "Oh, Doc, I can't drink that city water." He said, "Okay, I'll give you this other kind." He turned on the hot water spigot and got water from it for her. That was fine with her.

There was a situation where Dr. Roberts delivered a baby but it died. Naturally, the mother was distraught over the death of her baby. In his effort to console her, her husband said, "Don't worry honey. We'll get another one."

Dr. Roberts delivered a baby for a family on Morris Hill. He asked them if they had any diapers and somebody spoke up, "I think there's one around here somewhere."

A man from Wayne County who was employed in Indiana went to see Dr. Roberts when he was in Monticello. He told Doc he wanted to get married, and he wondered if he could get his blood test in Indiana where he was working and his fiancee' could get Dr. Roberts to do her blood test. Dr. Roberts said he thought that was okay, and then he asked, "When do you want to get married?" The man replied, "She wants to wait 'til Christmas but I thought along about squirrel season would be a good time."

Part of the requirement in filling out papers after the birth of a child is to indicate what number child in the family the newborn is. After delivering a baby to one family Dr. Roberts asked what number this was. The man said he didn't know. He had four or five by a previous marriage. His wife had four or five by a previous marriage. They had four or five together. He said to his wife, "You count 'em." She told him, "You count 'em." Finally, they called in the oldest daugther and told her to count them.

Once in the 1950´s when Dr. Roberts was making house calls, he stopped at Wright Machinery to buy gasoline for his Jeep Wagoneer and to visit a few minutes as often was his custom. While there, a man who lived in New Town was looking for a ride, and being the good neighbor, Doc kindly offered to give him a ride. As they talked, the man asked Doc where he had been, realizing that Doc had come from his part of town. "I´ve been in New Town at Harley Latham´s place," Doc replied. Harley Latham was a man of meager means who worked at the local oak flooring mill many hours each day to support his ever increasing family. Inquisitively the rider asked, "Well, what´s wrong with Harley, Doc?" In his usual witty tone Doc said, "Harley has had a miscarriage!"

The hitchhiker could only imagine that something bad had happened to his friend, not realizing Doc was talking about Harley´s wife. Still pondering the thought of Harley being sick, as he was getting out of Doc´s Jeep, Harley´s friend commented, "Doc, I knew Harley was working too hard up at that old mill."

One woman went in for an office visit. She was terribly nauseated and feeling bad. Dr. Roberts examined her, asked her several questions and then asked, "Could you be pregnant?" She replied, "Well, I have been exposed."

Dr. Roberts is able to respond in kind immediately to patients. One man came in and said, "How do you do Brudder Roberts?" He responded, "I´m fine. How are you Brudder Shelton?" A response like this is non threatening and builds rapport, causing the patient to see Dr. Roberts as a human being just like the patient. Instead of diminishing respect, respect and appreciation for him are enhanced by his "in kind" responses to patients.

Citizens' Appreciation

To know Dr. Mack Roberts is to know a man who has cared for the medical needs of people who represent the spectrum of human beings. The only distinction that he has ever made between his patients has been to determine which one was in the greatest need and to care for that person first. Beyond this, he has treated his patients as people of equal value and worth.

This attitude along with his delightful humor and wit have endeared him to all citizens of Wayne County, whether or not they were his patients. He is a man who does not think more highly of himself than he should as illustrated by his response when one citizen said, "Doc, I hear they're writin' a book about you."

"Yeah. It's terrible, isn't it?" was his immediate reply.

"There is no one in Wayne County who is more deserving of the honor of having a book written about him than Mack Roberts," was Estill Alexander's opinion, which has been echoed by hundreds of citizens in the county.[1] Part of Estill's strong positive feelings about Dr. Roberts are the result of the many kindnesses he showed to his mother, Bertha Fairchild Alexander, during eleven years of illness. He was willing to make house calls at any time during the day or night as well as to see her at his home. Earlier in her life, Dr. Roberts sent her a postcard when he was on vacation in Florida with this message, "Bertha, don't have one of your fits 'til I get back. I'll need the money!"

Elba Wilhite is another citizen who testifies to the extraordinary care that Dr. Roberts gives as a physician.

It's been said that having the ability to make friends is one of God's greatest gifts. It involves many things, but above all, the power of giving of oneself and appreciating whatever is noble and loving in another. Dr. Roberts has such a gift. He is a friend to all--from all walks of life. He and my late husband, Murph, were bank associates and close friends for many years. Dr. Roberts provided medical skill, helpful advice, and cheerful optimism as personal physician and friend. He was ready to lend a helping hand--go the extra mile--whether day or night.[2]

The concerns of the patient have been the most important thing to Dr. Roberts, and compassion has been his strong point. Concern for the patient often is as valuable and significant as the treatment itself. Dr. Roberts knew this intuitively, and this has contributed to the deep appreciation and admiration that people have for him.

Dr. Roberts gave Betty Waddle Tuttle her first job. She had been looking in vain for a job in 1935, during the Depression, and had about given up hope. He hired her as a clerk for the Wayne County Health Department. The office was located on the second floor of the Rankin building. Betty worked for him unitl he resigned to do his internship at St. Joseph's Hospital in Lexington, Kentucky in 1938.

Also working for Dr. Roberts in the Health Department were Edna Brooking, County Health Nurse, Hattie Hurt, Secretary, and Mabel Noe,

Clerk. When the weather was good and Wayne County one-room schools were in session Dr. Roberts and his staff would drive out as a group to those schools and vaccinate the children for typhoid and small pox.

Edna Brooking, a native of Brooksville, Kentucky, lived in Monticello from 1934-38. She was the County Nurse when Dr. Roberts became the County Health Officer. Edna recounted her first encounter with Dr. Roberts:

> I well remember first meeting him in the Health Office, which was in the Rankin Building. I was a stranger in a strange town, far from my home-had no idea what my "boss" would be like, or even if he would accept me. I was told by my supervisor that he might not accept me, which was his privilege![3]

Dr. Roberts ended his interview with Edna by saying, "I make one request of my nurse, that you do not wear knickers (pants now) in public."

Edna was puzzled by this request because she had spent three years as a student at Berea College where such attire was "taboo." Later she understood. Edna saw girls in town wearing knickers and was told they were girls of ill repute! "It was then I realized he was advising me as he would his own sister, which he did those four years!"

Edna summarized her experience and appreciation for Dr. Roberts in these words, "His professional skills, ethics, his devotion to the church, his family and fellowman was an inspiration to me, and I feel sure has been to many all during his life."[4]

Glenna Mae Catron remembers being invited to help him when he came to her school to give the children vaccinations. She was so short she had to stand on a tree stump to swab the arms of the students and the teachers. As the gentle natured Health Officer of Wayne County, Dr. Roberts provided the first encounter many children had with a physician.

A couple went to see Dr. Roberts, and he removed a growth from the man's eyelid and a mole from his wife's chin. The charge for the two services was $10. On another occasion after treatment and a prescription had been written he was asked, "How much do we owe you?" Dr. Roberts responded, "Hmm. Well, I'm running a special today. You don't owe me anything." The patient commented to him, "You'll surely have a great reward at the judgment." Dr. Roberts replied, "Well, I'd hate to be the richest man in the graveyard."

W. R. Denny has done several original oil paintings for Mack and Alma. When he delivered one of those paintings to them in the autumn of 1985, Dr. Roberts wanted to know how much he owed for the painting. W. R. said, "Don't you think it's time someone did something for you?"

"Nope," he retorted and insisted on paying for the painting.

This attitude and action by Dr. Roberts caused W. R. Denny to sum up his opinion of his doctor this way, "Mack is an upright, honest, Christian doctor. We, the patients, can never say enough or do enough to repay him for what he has done for us."

Neva Piercy speaks for many people in Wayne County when she says,

> One thing we personally know
> about Dr. Roberts is he is for the

poor people. You could call him any time whether you had a dime or not. When our oldest son was born, May 6, 1948, we didn't have the money at the time, but Dr. Roberts said that was okay. Pay me later and when we got our check from my husband's school he went in and paid him. To me there wasn't a better doctor for the poor people in Wayne County. He would come to your home day or night.[6]

    Many citizens of Wayne County refer to him as "our Doctor Roberts." What an expression of possessive affection! People feel like he is a part of them and treat him like a member of their families. He encourages this attitude by talking with patients in the first person plural: our, we, and us. The patients are confident that Dr. Roberts is on their side and that he is with them in whatever they are experiencing.

    Barnett Abbott expressed the opinions and feelings of many people when he wrote in a letter:

> We are so grateful to have had Doctor Roberts as our doctor and friend for so many years. He is just one of us and a part of our family. He has been a true example of one who knows the value and quality of life with those who are less fortunate than he, for anytime--day or night, regardless of weather, whether the need was small or great, rich or poor, money or nothing--he always answered the call. He was always pleasant and

never in such a hurry that he would not give a patient all the time needed. Dr. Roberts has given us a true lesson that "Love for others is evident through our actions." How well he has lived and known what Jesus meant when he said, "It is more blessed to give than to receive."[7]

Dr. Roberts' sense of humor with his patients creeps up everywhere. Lewis Kelley enjoys telling about an office visit when he was sick. Dr. Roberts asked, "What's wrong, Kelley?"

Lewis described his symptoms. Then Dr. Roberts asked, "Have you been bothered with this before?"

"Yes, I have."

"Well, you've got it again," was Dr. Roberts' reply and he gave him a shot.

Dr. Roberts is a humanitarian who cares about people. One fifth grade school teacher told me that through the years she has had several children from the same family in her class. Each one of these children told her that Dr. Roberts gave him $5 for Christmas.

Dr. Rankin was well-known for his frugality, even described as being "down right tight" when it came to spending money. Whenever anyone in Monticello approached Dr. Roberts for a charitable contribution, he would promise, "I'll give twice as much as Doc Rankin gave."

There are many examples of Dr. Roberts' generosity. He has treated patients and not charged them, bought groceries and delivered to families of his patients, established a college loan at Cumberland College, given carillon chimes to both the Elk Spring Valley Baptist Church and the First Baptist Church of Monticello. In addition he has been a faithful financial contributor to the Elk Spring Valley Baptist Church where he has been a member for nearly seventy years.

John Simmons, one of Dr. Roberts' colleagues in Monticello made these observations about him:

> Mack never said anything rough to anyone. He was eager to get a hospital in Monticello as much for the benefit of newborn babies as anything. He has been good to the hospital staff, and he taught me to treat people right and be kind to them. He has been kind and supportive to me. Mack kept his focus on practicing medicine and never did really venture out into other things. He had hobbies like his farm and garden and enjoyed traveling but the one thing he did was to practice medicine. [8]

Dr. Mack Roberts has survived well both personally and professionally in the cultural climate where he was born and reared. He understood intuitively and naturally the nature and character of the people of Wayne County. He has accepted people as they are and treated them as if they were his own family. Many of them have been his relatives, and most of his patients have been his own cultural family. He has known and loved them, cared for them, and "doctored" them for more than half a century.

The accounts I have recorded in this chapter show the mutual care, acceptance, and appreciation shared by Dr. Roberts and his patients. These patients give testimony that Wayne County is richer because Mack Roberts has practiced medicine there. When he dies he may be the richest man in the graveyard, richest in appreciation and admiration.

Notes

[1] Estill Alexander, Personal Letter, March 8, 1986.
[2] Elba Wilhite, Personal Letter, February 28, 1986.
[3] Edna Brooking DeLoach, Personal Letter, March 9, 1986.
[4] Ibid.
[5] W. R. Denney, Personal Letter, March 8, 1986.
[6] Neva Piercy, Personal Letter, March 10, 1986.
[7] Barnett Abbot, Personal Letter, April 10, 1986.
[8] Interview with Dr. John Simmons, March 15, 1986.

8
"A LOT OF 'EM GET PULLED TOO GREEN"

The religious convictions and interest of Rhodes and Rona Roberts not only were important to them but also had an impact on their children. Permeating their comprehension of life was the teaching that they were answerable to God for the lives they lived and that the biblical instructions of the ten commandments were solid rules by which their family ought to abide. Mack's parents' faith was evident to him by how they treated their fellow human beings. Because religious faith was an integral part of Mack's home environment, his faith developed naturally and has positively affected him throughout his life.

Church Membership

Riding five miles by horseback behind his dad to go to church was one of the first trips Mack took. He was three years old, and they rode over the mountain, and through the woods to the Big Springs Baptist Church in Burfield. Clear in Mack's mind is the beautiful green velvet dress he saw a girl his own age wearing at church that day. "That was the most beautiful thing I had ever seen," Mack said, referring to the dress. This was the beginning of Mack's consistent participation in church.

From Mack's tenth year of life he has attended the Elk Spring Valley Baptist Church where he made a public profession of faith as a Christian in his middle teen years. There are church leaders who believe that if people do not make a public commitment to be a Christian before their twelfth birthdays the decisions won't be made. Mack's opinion about churches, ministers, and teachers who urge young children to make public professions of faith is, "A lot of 'em get pulled too green, and then later you see them struggling and needing to repeat the decision."

Although Mack has lived in Monticello for the last fifty years, he has continued to drive five miles each Wednesday evening and twice on Sundays to participate in the services of the Elk Spring Valley Baptist Church. He has remained a member of this congregation throughout his life because it is home to him and he likes the people there. The congregation benefits from his financial support and he considers this to have been of more help to the church than any spiritual value that he has had to offer. He has taught a Sunday school class occasionally but has not accepted that as a regular responsibility because often his involvement with a patient on Sunday prevents him from being on time. Practically every Sunday he sees patients before and after church services, either at his home or theirs, depending upon their circumstances, illnesses, and needs.

Being a reserved man, Mack does not speak out in the business meetings of the church. Once when discussion was dragging about what action the congregation should take, someone suggested that a motion was needed, and Mack said, "I make a motion like that." There was a second, the vote was taken, and the issue resolved. This is the extent to which Mack expresses himself publicly in the business affairs of the congregation.

Mack has never served as a deacon in his church. The congregation does not consider him to be in charge of his own house because his wife, Alma, is a member of another denomination. I asked him if this attitude bothered him and he said, "It suits me fine. I don't like having to be in the limelight and up in front of people anyway. Besides, I'm in charge. They just don't know it."

When he was a member of the Building Committee, Mack insisted that they obtain the services of an architect to draw up plans for constructing an addition to the building. Most of the members on the committee didn't understand why they needed to waste money on an architect. They knew what type building they wanted. Why couldn't they just get together and build it? Mack wanted the congregation to get the best value for the money they were going to invest in a building. Because of the importance he placed on having an architect, Mack promised to pay the architect's fees. The offer was too good for the committee to reject. An architect was obtained and a tastefully designed building was constructed.

As a child, Mack remembers the preachers being long and loud. He is convinced that a preacher can say more in twenty-five minutes, if he is prepared, than the people can put into practice during the week. This is why he suggested an alarm be on the clock to ring automatically at 12:00 noon, but no action has been taken on his suggestion.

When one pastor who was sick described his symptoms over the telephone, Dr. Roberts told his pastor he would write a prescription for him. Later that day a church member went by Dr. Roberts' office to pick up the prescription and Dr. Roberts said, "Tell him to take this three times a day and to cut fifteen minutes off his sermon and he'll get better." The next Sunday the pastor told this story during his sermon and abided by the prescription, at least that day.

A few years ago during revival services at the Elk Spring Valley Baptist Church, someone called Mack during the middle of the week and asked, "Are you going to church tonight?"

"Nope, nope," Mack responded. "Got an hour Sunday night and an hour last night. Two hours ought to be enough for three nights."

During a time when the congregation was attempting to raise money for an organ, and the donations were coming in slowly, the pastor made a plea, "I can't believe that a congregation worth a million dollars can't raise $2,500 for a new organ." Following the worship service Mack said to his pastor, "Preacher, I think you underestimated our worth." That afternoon the pastor thought about Dr. Roberts' comment and began adding up the land holdings of the members of the congregation and discovered they were worth at least three or four million dollars. Doc was right. The pastor had underestimated their worth.

Religious History

Mack's religious history reveals that his faith in God is deeply rooted in the Bible and well integrated in his lifestyle. The parallels between his favorite portions of the Bible and his approach toward life are intriguing.

Biblical Themes

Mack's life has been permeated by hope, love, joy, and grace. These are major biblical themes that have been played out in his life. These and other themes are expressed in his dreams and his views of prayer, evil, and sin.

Optimism is one of Mack's major characteristics, and it is related to the theme of hope. Mack functions daily with the conviction that life will move along smoothly, but when it doesn't, he never feels trapped. He is convinced there is a way out of the difficulty or disappointment. His optimism and hope are tied to his desire to give a good account of himself.

Passing the test is Mack's greatest hope. The test he wants to pass is his accountability to God for the life he has lived. This hope is the flip side of the fear of failing and is tied to a significant experience in his life. Occasionally, Mack still dreams about examinations in medical school and these dreams are permeated with a fear of failing. The medical school administration failed twenty students each year and the students who failed as well as those who passed were never able to determine what the criteria was for failing or passing. The medical students often were degraded and berated in class. Medical school was a difficult, pressure filled, frightening experience for Mack. Many years after he was in private practice he would drive miles out of his way to avoid going by the University of Louisville Medical School when he was in the city. Further indication of hope in Mack's life is demonstrated in wishes he would like God to grant him. When I asked, "If God could grant you three wishes, what would they be?" Without pondering for a moment or batting an eye, he said, "Put the devil out of business. That would take care of the other two." Obvious in this response was his clever mind, his sense of humor, and his view of the cause of problems and pain in the world.

Mack is convinced that the sources of many problems in the world are sin and evil. He is certain there is plenty of evil in the world and that "it is getting worse." Human beings are the cause of much pain because of their sins, and Mack thinks the sin of unbelief is the worst sin a person can commit. He readily confesses that his two greatest sins are indifference and ingratitude. By indifference he means that he could be doing a lot more in the Lord's work than he is and by ingratitude he means he just accepts many positive things that come his way without ever acknowledging his gratitude to God. He also claims that his most persistent temptation is laziness. Here is evidence of the impact of the Protestant work ethic on Mack's life modeled for him in both of his parents. They worked hard throughout their lives, and a major portion of their work motivation was the conviction that hard work pleased God. Mack has compensated for his fear of laziness with his tendency to work day and night providing medical care for the people of Wayne County.

Although Mack considers a person's relationship to God to be important, how the relationship occurs and is maintained has an unexplainable quality to it. I asked him, "How does God function in your life?"

"I don't know. It's beyond me," was his immediate reply.

This gives expression to the mystery of God's involvement in people's lives. Mack is convinced that everybody is dependent on God for existence, health, life, home, family, and friends. The most important religious concept to Mack is that God cared enough to send his son, and the most important thing for people to learn is what God's will is and try to do it. At least part of God's will for us from Mack's perspective is to be our brother's keeper and to help people who are in need, both physically and spiritually. This has been the motto and the purpose statement of Mack's life because his reason for being a physician and the reason that he has practiced medicine has been to be of help to people physically and spiritually. He is convinced that when a person is helped in one area of life, he is benefited in all areas of life.

Prayer is the communication system between people and God. Prayer is communion with God, and it is a daily part of Mack's life as he prays at least two or three times each day. He observed that too often our approach in prayer is, "Thanking God for the blessings we have received and then asking Him for more." Mack prays for his family, for friends who are sick, for the leaders of the country, for the church, and for family members who are traveling. How often he prays depends on the illness or difficulty a person is having in addition to how worried Mack is--a surprising comment because most people do not see him as a worrier. Perhaps this reveals how well his prayer life helps him cope with his worries!

Biblical Favorites

A person's favorite Bible story, Scripture verse, and biblical character provide insight into how he lives out his relationship to God. I found the similarity between Mack's life and his biblical favorites to be interesting.

Mack's favorite Bible story is the account of Joseph and his brothers recorded in Genesis. Joseph's brothers had sold him into slavery and later Joseph came to have a prominent position in the Egyptian government. Between the lines of the story is the hint that Joseph fantasized about the time when he would be able to get even with his brothers. When Joseph's opportunity came his interest in gaining revenge had waned.

Mack especially enjoys the portion of the story when Joseph tricked his brothers by having a cup from the royal treasury placed in Benjamin's bag. As punishment Joseph kept Benjamin and sent the rest of the brothers back home to report to their father and to return bringing their father with them.

"I've always thought that was a pretty good way to handle them after the way they had treated Joseph."

Mack enjoyed Joseph making life difficult for his brothers but eventually treating them fairly. Fairness is an important quality in life for Mack, and siding with a sick child demonstrates his concern for fairness. This example shows the truth of Mack's favorite biblical story coming alive in him.

When I asked Mack which verse of Scripture was his favorite, he replied, "They're all good." When I pressed him to choose one as his favorite he concluded that John 3:16 was it, "For God so loved the world that he gave his only begotten son that whosoever believeth in him should not perish but might have everlasting life." This is his favorite verse because it expresses his conviction that, "Everybody was lost until Christ came." Mack believes that he and all Christians should live their lives in a way that communicates the love and forgiveness of God demonstrated in the life of Christ.

Jesus is Mack's favorite biblical character because of Jesus' love for people. Jesus' humility, simplicity, and intelligence enabled him to relate to and care for all people. In many ways Mack has emulated these characteristics in his life according to the observations and comments that family members, friends, and patients have made about him. Mack responds humbly that he has not emulated these characteristics nearly enough in his life.

Managing His Gifts

Mack views his vocation as a calling from God. "I enjoy being a doctor and I think I owe it to God to be a doctor as long as I am able because God gave me the ability to be a doctor." His philosophy of life is, "Serve the Lord. Serve the Lord by serving His people. As long as I can contribute to the welfare of the human race, I am obligated to do that. Besides this is what I like to do." Here is evidence that Mack's faith in God and his religious development have permeated his life, are well intergrated in his living, and have contributed significantly to why he is a physician and to how he practices medicine.

9

EACH ONE GETS A LITTLE BETTER

Erik Erikson, a world renowned student and teacher of human development, has analyzed the growth and development of human beings. The characteristic developed in each stage comes out of the tension with which the person wrestles at that junction in his life. Wisdom is the characteristic that comes with the stage of old age.[1]

Chronologically, Dr. Mack Roberts is in old age, being eighty-three at the time of this writing. Being four score and three is the only sign that he is in the stage of old age, except for his outstanding wisdom that often is communicated with a pinch of humor.

His philosophy of life is, "Sit level in the saddle." He is especially fond of one of Mark Twain's comments. Twain was asked what he would do if he had only thirty days to live. Twain responded, "I'd take it a day at a time."

Community Affairs

Dr. Roberts has been active in community affairs in addition to being a doctor to people throughout the county. He has served on the board of directors of the Monticello Banking Company for the past 37 years and has served as President of the bank since 1978. He is a past President of the Wayne County Hospital Executive Board of Physicians, a member of the Wayne County Medical Association, the Kentucky Medical Association, and the American Medical Association. He is a member of Theta Kappa Psi Medical Fraternity, the Society of Gideons, and an active member of Elk Spring Valley Baptist Church.

Although Dr. Roberts is best known and appreciated for his medical practice, he has not been a one dimensional citizen. He has contributed to the welfare of Wayne County citizens through his medical practice, his church involvement, and the business practices of the Monticello Banking Company.

Storyteller

Often it is common of people who have a delightful sense of humor not only to enjoy collecting stories but also to be excellent storytellers. Dr. Roberts has a wealth of Wayne County folklore stored in his mind, and it comes flowing out in general conversation and when he is driving along the country roads on his way to make house calls. The following stories about Aus Brown and Will Duncan are two I heard him recount that I found delightful and typical of the yarns that he enjoys spinning.

Aus Brown was a lawyer in Wayne County who lived in Duncan Valley. He was a representative in the State Legislature on one occasion, and a book was written about him under the title <u>Damn Fool in the State Legislature</u>. Aus had a reputation for hoarding money, being stingy with what he had, and searching for ways to improve his situation financially with little regard for the result or impact his action might have on anyone else.

One of Aus' clients was in serious trouble and had been brought to trial. After the evidence had been presented, the judge studied the case. Then Aus, representing his client, went to hear the ruling from the judge. After hearing the ruling, Aus stopped by his client's house to give him a report. Aus told his client that the judgment had gone against him. The client asked, "What should I do?"

"The best thing for you to do is to leave the country, and you'd better leave tonight." Aus bought the man's farm that night at a bargain price.

The second story also involves a lawsuit. Will Duncan filed suit to recover financial losses and he had itemized several losses in the suit. One of his claims was $500 for a dry hole that had been drilled in search of oil. The lawyer for the defendant questioned Will about the claim for a dry hole and asked, "How can a dry hole be worth anything?"

"It tells you where not to drill," was Will's immediate reply.

Health Care

Dr. Roberts' physical, mental, and emotional health continue to be excellent. The sickest he claims ever to have been was the reaction he had to a small pox vaccination. The only serious health problem he has had over the years was some difficulty with angina in 1960 which has been corrected. His blood pressure does get a little bit high on occasion. When that happens, he takes some medication. To monitor his health he goes to Lexington for his "annual" physical about every three years.

He denies having had any great success but attributes what success he has had to being on the job. People throughout Wayne County can testify to the validity of the statement that he has been on the job because they have called on him for medical care all hours of the day and night in all seasons and all kinds of weather and no one has been refused treatment, regardless of how minor the need might seem. A person's health need is never minor to the person. Dr. Roberts understands that and takes seriously whatever the concern of the patient is that he is seeing at the moment.

Wit

In the spring of 1986 Rick and Marilyn Drake purchased a houseboat. They were not sure how Mack and Alma would respond to this purchase. Alma is uncomfortable around the water and is fearful of her children and grandchildren spending time on the lake. Mack does not have the same fears, but apparently Marilyn had some concern about his reaction because when the Drakes were ready to inform him about the purchase they decided to let their son deliver the message. Just before little Mack told the news, Marilyn said, "Daddy, you better brace yourself." To which he responded, "I stay braced." He received the news about the houseboat well and has enjoyed several trips on it. He stays braced.

Having been a home owner for more than four decades and having been involved with each of his daughters and sons-in-law as they have become home owners, Dr. Roberts has one bit of advice for every home owner, "You can never fix a leak."

I mentioned in chapter four about the vast difference in Mack and Alma's denominational affiliation. Although that has been a source of disagreement at times, it also has provided opportunities for some comic relief, usually as a result of his comments. He has said on more than one occasion, "There's nothing wrong with the Church of Christ that a good organ wouldn't cure." In 1970 the Oil Valley Church of Christ built a new building and Alma gave most of the money for the construction. Many people in the county knew this and someone asked Dr. Roberts,

"What are you going to give to the new Oil Valley Church of Christ?"

"I think I'll give the instruments," was his dry response.

Alma in turn has said, "We'll take the money."

When Mack was six years old his mother walked out on the porch where they lived and said, "There's Halley's Comet." She pointed it out to him and he was able to see it for three consecutive nights. He described it as, "A bright star followed by a long trail of light." He was eager to see it in 1986 and said, "I'd like to see it at least two or three more times before I die."

Many changes have occurred in the world and in Wayne County during the past fifty years. Transportation methods have changed from Model T's and Model A's to a variety of styles and speeds of automobiles, from single engine prop airplanes to huge jetliners that can cross the nation quicker than a person could go from Monticello to Cincinnati in 1930. One thing that has remained constant has been the medical care provided for citizens of Wayne County by Mack Roberts. He is known affectionately by practically everyone in Wayne County as "Doc" Roberts.

In 1983, in honor of Dr. Roberts' eightieth birthday, city and county officials declared July "Dr. Mack Roberts Month." The citation for "Dr. Mack Roberts Month" read: "Dr. Mack is known to his family and close friends as a quiet, gentle man with a quick, dry wit, who has great love for and pride in his family, his profession, his community and his country." Congressman Harold Rogers read a statement about Dr. Roberts and had it included in the Congressional Record.

On his eightieth birthday and the declaration of Mack Roberts' month, Dr. Roberts commented about his birthday that "each one of them gets a little better." That continues to be his philosophy as he sits level in the saddle.

The title "Doc" is never more warmly used than when the citizens of Wayne County, Kentucky, use it to refer to Mack Roberts. He has lived his life a day at a time grateful to God for the gift of life he has received and for the ability he has been given to care for people's health needs. He has been a faithful steward of his life and abilities. He has brought sunshine to hundreds of homes when darkness and despair had engulfed them. He is deeply loved by his family, greatly appreciated by his patients, and fondly admired by the citizens of Wayne County. I hope this book not only has enabled you to know Doc but also has provided you with insight and wisdom that will cause you to say on your birthday, "Each one gets a little better."

Notes

[1] Erik H. Erikson, <u>Childhood and Society</u>, (New York: W. W. Norton & Company, Inc., 1950), p. 268.

Dr. Mack Roberts.

BIBLIOGRAPHY

Books

Erikson, Erik H. <u>Childhood and Society</u>. New York: W. W. Norton & Company, Inc., 1950.

Johnson, Augusta Phillips. <u>A Century of Wayne County Kentucky 1800-1900</u>. Louisville: The Standard Printing Company, 1939.

Articles

Jones, Linda. "Dr. Roberts' Birthday Is Celebrated by County." (Monticello, Kentucky: <u>The Wayne County Outlook</u>, Vol. 80, No. 10, July 28, 1983), pp. 1-2.